P9-DIY-783

Take-Away
APPLIQUÉ

Take-Away
APPLIQUÉ

To Fran —
What fun to be with
you in Paducah! Have
a great time with your
applique!
Best wishes,
Suzanne Marshall
4/21/99

by
SUZANNE MARSHALL

American Quilter's Society
P. O. Box 3290 • Paducah, KY 42002-3290

Located in Paducah, Kentucky, the American Quilter's Society (AQS), is dedicated to promoting the accomplishments of today's quilters. Through its publications and events, AQS strives to honor today's quiltmakers and their work—and inspire future creativity and innovation in quilt-making.

EDITOR: MARY JO KURTEN
TECHNICAL EDITOR: BARBARA SMITH
BOOK DESIGN/ILLUSTRATIONS: ELAINE WILSON
COVER DESIGN: TERRY WILLIAMS
PHOTOGRAPHY: CHARLES R. LYNCH, UNLESS INDICATED OTHERWISE
PRINTED IN THE U.S.A. BY IMAGE GRAPHICS INC., PADUCAH, KY

Library of Congress Cataloging-in-Publication Data
Marshall, Suzanne.
    Take-away Appliqué / by Suzanne Marshall.
       p. cm.
    ISBN 1-57432-706-2
      1. Appliqué — Patterns.   2. Quilting Patterns.   I. Title.
TT779.M285   1998
746.46'041--dc21   98-2724
                                                    CIP

Additional copies of this book may be ordered from: American Quilter's Society, PO Box 3290, Paducah, KY 42002-3290 @ $22.95. Add $2.00 for postage & handling.

Copyright © 1998, Suzanne Marshall

This book or any part thereof may not be reproduced without the written consent of the author and publisher. Exception: the authors and publisher give permission to photocopy pages 73, 74, 84–88, 94, 95, 103, 105–107, 113, 114, 116–120, 122–168 for personal use only. The information and patterns in this book have been provided in good faith. The American Quilter's Society has no control of materials or methods used and, therefore, is not responsible for the use of or results obtained from this information.

This book is dedicated to my parents,

Marjorie and Kenneth Russell

ITALIAN WINE MAKING, 28" x 34", 1995.
Adapted from the *Tacuinum Sanitatis*, this quilt
was made as a special gift for my father on his
84th birthday.

contents

CASS GILBERT REMEMBERED (detail facing
page). Full quilt shown on page 34.

introduction

Never in my wildest dreams would I have imagined that checking out a library book to help me make a quilt for our daughter would lead to years of quilt-making and eventually writing this book. My first pathetic quilts were utilitarian, increasing in size as the children grew. Only after I started making appliqué quilts did I discover the fun and excitement of making the quilts more personal by adding details from trips and incorporating historical images that spoke to me from the past. It is my hope that others will be inspired to make quilts with more personal meaning after reading this book.

As a self-taught quiltmaker, I tried techniques by trial and error and did a lot of experimenting—never being sure if I was doing things right. I made many mistakes, but just kept going. In the process, I developed some methods that worked for me, and I hope they will be useful to other quiltmakers.

Making quilts without instruction, I began wondering what I was doing right and what I was doing wrong. I figured a good way to get feedback was to try for a national quilt competition, see if my quilts could get juried in, and then hopefully learn from the judges' critiques. Luckily, I was juried into the first competition that I entered and even won a top prize! The critiques were helpful, and I applied some of the suggestions to future quilts. Included in this book are judges' comments, both positive and negative, for the quilts that have been entered in competitions. You can look at a picture of the quilt and then decide if you agree with the comments. It is also apparent that judges don't necessarily agree. It is interesting to receive contradictory statements from different judges. It is also possible to receive negative comments and still win a top prize.

My husband, Garland, deserves a lot of credit. He goes to work with threads hanging from his clothes and has even found pins and needles in the bed. He's still supportive! He loves to critique my quilts as I make them. Sometimes I pay attention to what he says, but other times I feel like I have to go my own way. As I started writing this book, he began making suggestions, "Why don't you say this?" or "Be sure and include that." I said, "Why don't you add your comments to the book? That way you can give your own perspective and your voice will be heard. You express yourself differently than I do anyway." So, that's what happened.

Looking at my quilts hanging in a retrospective show, I realize that I have definitely learned a lot since my first quilt. Every quilt I have made has taught me a lesson to apply to another quilt, and often, one thing leads to another. While I'm working on a quilt, ideas for another start bubbling around in my head, often incorporating some technique or idea from the previous quilt. The quilts in this book are primarily presented in the order that I made them, so that you can see the evolution of my quiltmaking.

My quilts usually start with one idea. I don't plan the whole quilt ahead of time. I may start appliquéing something that may be the center of a quilt and then build out from that. Or I may make enough squares for a quilt without having a clue as to how to put them together or what the border will look like. In many ways, quiltmaking is like gardening. First you plant a seed. It germinates and has possibilities but has a long way to go. It keeps developing and changing. Then it produces a bud with the promise of a flower. What will the flower look like when it blooms? What will the quilt look like when it's finished? It's exciting to see how a quilt develops from "seed" to "flower."

During my retrospective exhibits, I have demonstrated how to quilt without a hoop or a frame. Many of the onlookers were fascinated, wishing that they could try to quilt the same way. "But you're breaking all of the rules," I was told. "I don't know what the rules are!" I replied. The methods that I have included in this book were developed on my own. I have no idea if they follow the rules or if there is a better way. I simply know that this is what works for me, and if these methods help you in making your quilts, that makes me happy.

At the end of the book, I have included some patterns and design motifs from some of my quilts. You are welcome to incorporate them in something you are making if they appeal to you. The lampposts in front of the St. Louis Art Museum contain images of squirrels, which I have used in four different quilts. This shows that the same design motif can be used in several ways from one quilt to another.

Most of all, I hope you enjoy the process of quiltmaking—the actual doing of it. The resulting quilt or a prize in a contest is simply a bonus.

Tacuinum Sanitatis, Natural History magazine. COURTESY OF THE
SPENCER COLLECTION, THE NEW YORK PUBLIC LIBRARY, ASTOR, LENOX
AND TILDEN FOUNDATION.

TAKE-AWAY APPLIQUÉ

The Beginning

Plate 1-1. PINWHEEL QUILT, 36" x 65", 1976.

I grew up in southwest Missouri and wore clothes my mother made for me. I can remember going to the feed store with my father to pick out material for my next dress, because many of my clothes were made out of feed sacks. Scraps from my feed-sack dresses were later sewn into a crazy-quilt skirt for me to wear. My father created a zany, colorful length of cloth that my mother sewed into an eye-catching full skirt. Pennies were scarce in those days, but I had a new skirt in spite of tough economic times, and, wow, did that skirt ever attract attention! The only thing I didn't like about it was that people lifted my skirt to see the underside and look at its construction!

Store-bought clothes were beyond my wildest dreams. During my high school years, I worked in the summer, typing for college students so I could earn the money to buy a sewing machine of my own to take to college with me.

In 1976, I began wondering what to do with all of the accumulated fabric scraps I had saved through the years. I decided it might be fun to try making a quilt, but had no idea how to go about it, and didn't know anyone at that time who made quilts. Nor did I know that a quilt revival was beginning.

Since our four children needed covers on their beds, that gave me the incentive to visit the public library and look at the quilting books. I found a pinwheel quilt pattern which seemed like a good choice for using my scraps of fabric. I cut templates out of an old cereal box and got started. The finished quilt was fairly small, because I grew tired of putting the same pattern together over and over again. (Plate 1-1)

But maybe the *Pinwheel Quilt* wasn't my first quilt after all. A few years earlier, our son Keith needed a resting mat to take to nursery school with him. Remembering my crazy-quilt skirt that my parents had made for me when I was a child, I gathered some scraps together and made a resting mat, inspired by a picture in a magazine. Possibly, the satisfaction of completing the little lion mat motivated me to look at my scrap collection in a different way and propelled me toward quiltmaking. (Plate 1-2)

Looking back at my early quilts, I realize that they were small, about the size of our children. They had little quilting on them. I was more fascinated with making blocks and arranging them in a different way. I was determined to make a quilt as long as a child's bed, so another early quilt, based on a star pattern, is distinguished by minimal quilting and a very strange size (40" x 81"). In fact, if our son rolled over in bed, he found he didn't have a quilt covering him anymore.

One April, all four of our children took turns with a virus. I put little fan patterns together for the Mohawk Trails pattern while I was playing games with the children. The scraps from our daughter's dresses and nightgowns, plus some of my maternity dresses went into the Mohawk Trails quilt. This quilt, however, is called *April Virus* in our family. (Plate 1-3)

The quilts that I made in the late '70s and early '80s were all made out of scraps and remnants. They were used by our four children on their beds and increased in size as the children grew. Most of them are now entirely worn out—full of tattered pieces of cloth with ink stains from homework. It makes me happy that they were used and loved, and I think it gave the children an appreciation for quilts that they might not have if they hadn't slept under them every

Plate 1-2. LION MAT, 38" x 46", 1971.
PHOTO: SUZANNE MARSHALL

Plate 1-3. APRIL VIRUS, 62" x 80", 1978.
PHOTO: SUZANNE MARSHALL

night and seen me working on them daily.

The children were sometimes included in the design process. Our son Keith designed a *King's Crown* quilt by coloring squares on graph paper. I quilted the top very little. He took it with him to the university, and I haven't seen it since, although he says he still has it. (Plate 1-4)

My husband started a company named Tripos in 1979, and I made a quilt for the office that blended beautifully with a new carpet in the room. It was patterned after an Amish quilt that I saw pictured in a book and was made out of squares and triangles and set in the barn-raising design. We hung the quilt, and I felt proud of it. Not long afterward, my husband hired a man to run the company, and the next thing I knew, the

Plate 1-4. KING'S CROWN, 73" x 73", 1970s.

quilt was taken down, folded up, and stored in a closet. I, therefore, named the quilt *Tripos Reject*. (Plate 1-5)

When our oldest son, Chris, left for college, I made a quilt called *Ice Blocks* for him out of baby blocks. I hated parting with the quilt, so I ended up making one for us, too. It now hangs in our dining room. (Plate 1-6, page 16)

Making the same quilt block over and over can get monotonous, so I had fun making different patterns for a sampler quilt. I didn't realize I was going to have a whole quilt when I started. I was just trying different patterns. (Plate 1-7, page 17)

A basket quilt filled with oranges was my first attempt at appliqué. I had a dreadful time with it, because I didn't know to use

Plate 1-5. TRIPOS REJECT, 79" x 79", 1983.

100-percent cotton for the appliqué. I wondered why the edges were so difficult to crease and hold a fold.

Learning by trial and error is certainly the slow way, but eventually the message came through. The *President's Wreath* quilt that I made for my parents' 50th wedding anniversary convinced me. The green fabric was a polyester/cotton blend, and the red flowers were appliquéd with 100-percent cotton. I could definitely tell the difference. (Plate 1-8, page 18)

Plate 1-6. ICE BLOCKS, 54" x 86", 1983.

Plate 1-7. SAMPLER, 52" x 79", 1984.

Plate 1-8. PRESIDENT'S WREATH, 80" x 96", 1982.

The
Transition
and
Beyond

BALTIMORE ALBUM SAMPLER

In 1984, a transition occurred in my quilt-making. My husband, Garland, gave me a gift certificate to purchase brand new fabric for use in a quilt. He said he'd like to see me make a quilt without using scraps and remnants. It seemed so extravagant to buy fabric for a quilt instead of using my accumulated scraps, but I must admit that he gave me the push I needed to go in a different direction.

I had seen pictures of old Baltimore Album quilts in books and knew that I wanted to try to make one. Since there weren't any patterns out at that time (and since I don't like purchasing patterns for quilts anyway), I started drawing some simple 18" blocks for a *Baltimore Album Sampler*. I turned in my gift certificate for brand new red and green 100-percent cotton (thank goodness I had learned that lesson).

Not being sure how to do all of that appliqué, I tried all kinds of methods. First I tried ironing the edges down around a cardboard template. That was tedious and I burned myself about a dozen times. Then I tried basting the edges down, but when I tried sewing the appliqué to the background, the edges weren't smooth and my points were nonexistent. I tried marking the background and then turning the edges under on the appliqué to match the markings. That didn't work for me either. But by this time I'd actually made a couple of squares.

Determined to find a way to master the technique, I finally drew around the template onto the front of the fabric to be appliquéd, eye-balled a ¼" turn-under allowance and cut the piece out, basted the piece in place, and painstakingly needle turned the edges. I found the ¼" edge I had cut to turn under was too bulky, so I cut that back closer to ⅛" as time went by. It was mighty slow-going at first, but at least I could forget the iron and concentrate on one stitch at a time. This eventually worked for me, and every time I see the quilt (which hangs in our living room), I can see my "history" of mastering appliqué on one quilt.

THOUGHTS FROM GARLAND:

Little did I know what I was encouraging. Already, I must have had some suspicions that Suzanne had an artistic bent. Being constrained to work in scraps was clearly limiting her creative talents. Besides, she seemed more interested in making quilts than in making clothes, which had been the source of scraps. It's a decision that I have never regretted, and I actually enjoy going fabric shopping with her to help encourage her to add to her collection. It's quite apparent that her ability to realistically portray animals, insects, etc., is dependent on the right fabric being available when she's ready to appliqué.

One lesson which I think is apparent from Suzanne's experience is that there is no one correct way to make a quilt. Since she has never taken a class, she has had to discover the way that works best for her. In being free to explore alternatives, she has discovered some approaches which may be novel, some of which were probably known and not transmitted in an organized way, and rediscovered some which may have become disfavored as organized quilting has become a force. What seems to be important is that you find a method that satisfies the technical aspect of quiltmaking and allows you to explore your own creativity. After all, if you're going to spend several months on a quilt project, making the design your own expression is in order.

Plate 2-1. BALTIMORE ALBUM SAMPLER, 86" x 86", 1984.

BY HEART AND HAND

After finishing the *Baltimore Album Sampler*, I still had a lot of red and green fabric left over. Once again, that meant I could use scraps and remnants in another quilt! The St. Louis Art Museum had a special exhibit of folk art in 1984, and I fell madly in love with a Whig's Defeat quilt that I saw in the exhibition. Part of it was printed on the exhibit brochure, so that helped me to draw out the pattern. All of the pieces were painstakingly cut out individually and sewn together one by one for *By Heart and Hand*. (At that time there was no paper piecing that I knew about.) I added diamonds at the top and the bottom so that it would fit better on the bed.

Plate 2-2. BY HEART AND HAND, 77" x 87", 1985.

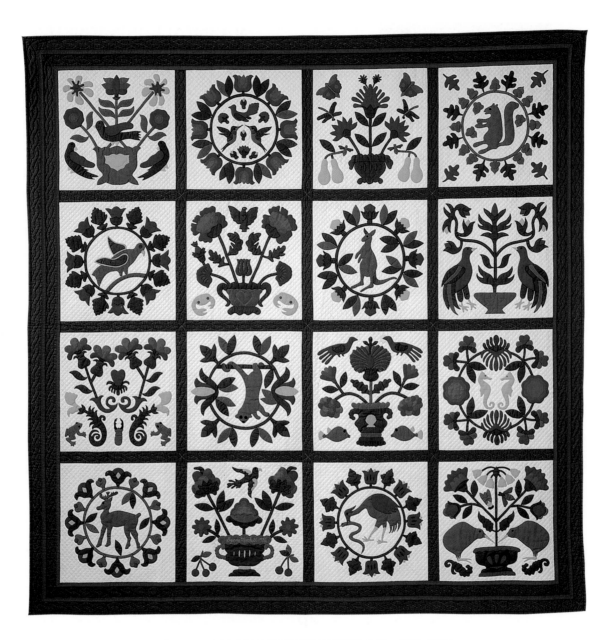

Plate 2-3. MARSHALL MENAGERIE, 86" x 86", 1986.

Plate 2-4. Mosaic floor from St. Mark's Cathedral, Venice, Italy. PHOTO: SUZANNE MARSHALL

Plate 2-5. Another mosaic floor from St. Mark's Cathedral. PHOTO: SUZANNE MARSHALL

MARSHALL MENAGERIE

After piecing all of those little bitty diamonds, I was ready to get back to appliqué. I came across a book called *American Graphic Quilt Designs* by Dolores A. Hinson (c. 1983) and found a picture of an early Baltimore-style quilt made around 1850 by Rachel Meyer. It had animals, birds, and flowers on it, and that appealed to me.

I decided to try making a similar Baltimore quilt, but this time, I added animals, birds, fish, and insects that reminded our family of different trips and experiences that we have had together.

The kangaroo brings to mind our trip to Australia. The square with the kiwi birds (lower right corner) reminds us of the year we lived in New Zealand when my husband was on sabbatical there. The kinkajou (row three, second square from left) was a pet that we had before we started our family. We also had a saltwater aquarium with a puffer fish in it. It eventually ate everything else in the tank and was so tame we could feed it by hand. Seahorses remind us of the scuba diving trips we have taken to Bonaire. The crabs make us think of our beachcombing walks and our love of the ocean. The squirrels have practically taken over our yard in St. Louis.

THOUGHTS FROM GARLAND:

A most interesting episode occurred during a visit to Washington, D.C., in association with the opening of the Healing Legacies exhibit at the U.S. House of Representatives. We went to the Renwick Gallery, the crafts part of the Smithsonian across from the White House. While browsing in their gift shop, I heard a cry of alarm from Suzanne. Six of her blocks from Marshall Menagerie had been reproduced in a book with copyright-free patterns from Baltimore Album quilts without her knowledge or permission. Eventually, after considerable effort, the publisher agreed to give Suzanne credit for her designs in future printings of the book. What is ironic is that Suzanne would have been so flattered to have her designs included in the first place that she would readily have given permission if asked.

I'll never forget our youngest son, Lee, trying to catch frogs one summer. And the various birds represent our fascination with them. We have feeders near the window next to our breakfast table.

Two squares were patterned after floor mosaics in St. Mark's Cathedral in Venice. See Plates 2-4 and 2-5, page 24.

Marshall Menagerie has won several prizes around the country, and I learned from the judges that, in order to improve the quilt, I should have more quilting in the appliqué to provide relief. I could go back and add more quilting, but I believe this quilt is part of my history the way it is, and I would prefer to leave it as I made it in 1986.

I have made a few wallhangings using several squares from the *Marshall Menagerie* quilt as centers. The pattern for the last square on the second row (Love Birds) begins on page 102.

THE SOUL OF MEDIEVAL ITALY

In 1963, we received a *Natural History* magazine that I found very difficult to throw away. Every time we packed up and moved or I sorted through magazines to recycle, I kept this one. It contained an article (Karl Kup, "A Medieval Codex of Italy," *Natural History*, December 1963, pp. 31-41) (Plate 2-6) about a manuscript of the *Tacuinum Sanitatis* which was written in a northern Italian dialect and illustrated during the 15th century with simple scenes from the lives of the Italian people. Something about those 15th-century drawings grabbed me, and I couldn't part with the magazine. At that time, I had never even contemplated making a quilt and had never been to Italy.

Twenty-five years later, I was quilting

and had been to Italy several times. I came across the magazine again, and it sang to me. On New Year's Day 1987, I photocopied and enlarged the drawings, trying to adapt each one to a 19" x 22" block. Who knows why I settled on that particular dimension!

I started with the magazine cover. Feeling satisfied once the appliqué was done, I plowed through the rest of the drawings. I had no idea how to appliqué trees, so I tried making them by trial and error, appliquéing them differently in many of the blocks. After all, I felt like I was experimenting more than anything else, and if a quilt evolved along

Plate 2-6. Cover of *Natural History* magazine, December 1963, with an article about the *Tacuinum Sanitatis.* COURTESY OF THE SPENCER COLLECTION, THE NEW YORK PUBLIC LIBRARY, ASTOR, LENOX AND TILDEN FOUNDATION.

Plate 2-7. THE SOUL OF MEDIEVAL ITALY, 71" x 79", 1987.

Take-Away Appliqué

the way, great! (Drawings from the *Tacuinum Sanitatis* can be found on pages 10, 76, and 108.)

The appliqué adapted from the *Natural History* magazine cover is in the top row, center, of *The Soul of Medieval Italy* (Plate 2-7).

The month that I finished the quilt, we learned that our daughter, Melissa, would be an AFS student the following year in the same part of northern Italy where the original manuscript was written. The quilt will be hers.

The Soul of Medieval Italy has won awards in Missouri and Indiana, at the American Quilter's Society show in Paducah, Kentucky, and the Woodlawn Plantation, and it was in an invitational exhibit in the Museum of American Folk Art in New York City.

In the competitions where the quilt won awards, I received both negative and positive comments. I have gathered all of the remarks and share them with you. Remember, I didn't get all of these critiques at once. Thank goodness I didn't have to read all of the negative comments at one time!

A few years ago, my husband and I visited New York City and I decided I would love to see the original *Tacuinum Sanitatis* that is kept under lock and key in the Spencer Collection at the New York Public Library. In order to see this valuable manuscript, one must fill out an application, have references,

NEGATIVE COMMENTS
too much green for my taste
designs a bit heavy
pencil marks
marks must be removed; at your level of expertise, visible markings are disappointing (I felt like I had been spanked when I read that one.)
binding should be narrower
would a stronger border have framed it more effectively (I must admit I tried a fancy geometric border on it and didn't like it because I felt like it detracted from the scenes on the quilt.)
shadowing (I had no idea what that meant and had to do a bit of research to learn that I had appliquéd a light color over a dark color and hadn't cut out behind it so the darker color showed through the light color.)

POSITIVE COMMENTS
beautifully executed
wonderful detailing
colors are well pleasing (I guess that judge likes green.)
outstanding color, design, and technique (Another judge likes green.)
rich, vibrant color effectively carries chosen design (What can I say; I like green, too!)

Plate 2-8. Original illustration from *Natural History* magazine, December 1963, from an article about the *Tacuinum Sanitatis*. Courtesy of the Spencer Collection, The New York Public Library, Astor, Lenox and Tilden Foundation.

THOUGHTS FROM GARLAND:

I was beginning to realize that Suzanne had creative abilities that were far beyond simply making quilts for our bed. Her response to the *Tacuinum Sanitatis* pictured in the *Natural History* magazine reflects a deep identification with folk and primitive art. The *Tacuinum Sanitatis*, or Tables of Health, is a text of dietetics, hygiene, and domestic medicine compiled in the second half of the 11th century by a Christian physician, Abu-l-Hasan al-Mukhtar ibn al-Hasan ibn Abdun ibn Sa'dun ibn Butlan, living in Baghdad. It is considered a milestone in the history and development of man's knowledge. Only a few illustrated manuscripts of this text from the Middle Ages exist in Paris, Vienna, Liege, Rouen, the Vatican, and the Spencer Collection. Based on the text, the version in the Spencer Collection is almost surely a copy of the one in Vienna, but with dramatic changes. The formal Latin text is now in a northern Italian dialect (probably from the area around Verona, the setting for *Romeo and Juliet*). The elegant gouaches of proud knights and court ladies are replaced by simple illustrations of the common man, whether peasant or tradesman. Had the article focused on one of the versions showing life at court, I doubt seriously if the illustrations would have caught Suzanne's attention.

list publications, and have an interview. I also wrote a letter to the curator and sent a picture of the quilt. During our interview, the sophisticated New Yorker wanted to know why we wanted to see the manuscript, being used to Ph.D. candidates and academic requests. He didn't quite know how to respond when I said I had made a quilt based on the illustrations.

But we did get to see the manuscript! The librarian was excited about bringing it out from its protection, because she says it is rare for the curator to allow people to look at it due to its age and value. She made a platform covered with velvet for it to rest on while we looked at it. Someday, I hope to make another quilt based on some of the other illustrations that we were allowed to photograph.

MIRACLES

In our local public library, there is a book called *Needlework in America; History, Designs, and Techniques* by Virginia Churchill Bath. It contains a drawing adapted from an embroidered bedcover made by a 19-year-old girl named Mary Breed. I had never tried making a medallion quilt, so I thought it might work to use one of the embroidery motifs as the center of a quilt.

I started the appliqué without having an inkling of an idea where it would take me, but I made sure that the center panel was a dimension on both sides that would be divisible by three inches. That way, if I decided to use patchwork borders, the math would be much easier when finding patterns to fit around all four sides. After finishing the appliqué on the medallion, I was faced with the problem of what to do next.

Searching the pattern books, I found several patchwork designs that I liked and made short sample pieces to try next to the center. Each border was decided on only after finishing the previous border. That way the entire quilt was a surprise to me when it was finished.

I named the quilt *Miracles* because the gray tones of the quilt remind me of winter, and the center design with the tree, birds, and leaves reminds me of the "miracles" of spring as it arrives and brings color to a gray winter world.

Miracles is the first quilt that I entered in a national competition. Since I am a self-taught quiltmaker, I was curious to see if it could be juried into a show so that I could receive critiques from the judges to learn what I was doing wrong. I was very excited when *Miracles* was juried into the Quilter's Heritage Celebration, Lancaster, Pennsylvania, in 1988, and I was shocked to learn that it won a blue ribbon. Sure enough, the judges' critiques were helpful, because they told me that my faint quilting lines showed. I ended up throwing the quilt in the washing machine when I got home to see if the pencil marks would come out. I was very nervous about washing it, because I was worried that the red berries might bleed, even though I had prewashed the fabric. But it worked! The pencil lines came out, and the next time I entered the quilt in a competition it won Best of Show.

Miracles has won top awards in Pennsylvania, Illinois, Missouri, Texas, and Montana, and has been in six invitational exhibits around the country. The judges' critiques for all of the competitions are on page 30.

The stars in *Miracles* were sewn together with a seam between the two stars. One of the judges at an exhibit where the quilt won Best of Show walked me over to the quilt and pointed out that the judges would have preferred for me to eliminate the seam between the two stars. It was only because my piecing was precise that the seam was not noticeable.

I wish I had thought of sewing the stars the way the judges suggested. It would have made the piecing a lot easier!

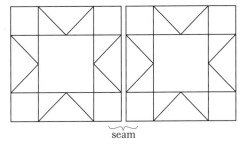

Fig. 2-1a. Method I used for sewing stars together.

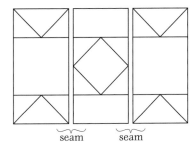

Fig. 2-1b. Suggested way to sew borders of stars.

THOUGHTS FROM GARLAND:

I believe that Mary Breed was associated with Breed's Hill in Boston, where the monument commemorating the Battle of Bunker Hill stands. We also visited the Metropolitan Museum on our trip to New York City and were wandering through the American Wing when, much to our amazement, we turned the corner and faced the original bed cover, which Suzanne recognized immediately. We had no idea that the bed cover was part of their collection and knew that most of the collection is seldom on display because of a lack of space. What a treat to think about this young woman during the revolutionary period making her treasures for her dowry and the response that her work has generated so many years later.

Plate 2-9. Mary Breed's "crewel work" bedspread (1770) embroidered in wool on linen; the flowers, leaves and some berries are in "oriental" or "Roumanian" stitch, four principal stems in a variety of herringbone stitch. PHOTO COURTESY: THE METROPOLITAN MUSEUM OF ART, ROGERS FUND, 1922. (22.55)

NEGATIVE COMMENTS

visual pencil lines

border tends to overwhelm center medallion

don't feel borders relate to center section, especially the middle one

binding should be filled with batting

piecing could be more precise (See the first positive comment.)

POSITIVE COMMENTS

precision piecing nice (So who's right?)

quilting shows up wonderful on back

quilting design fits and fills all areas

embroidery on birds adds to effect

visual appeal great

excellent use of limited color palette

dimensions in gray very good

embroidery enhances design

circles and curves handled extremely well

elegant overall appearance

Plate 2-10. MIRACLES, 78" x 91", 1988.

CASS GILBERT REMEMBERED

One day I had a luncheon engagement with a friend of mine at the St. Louis Art Museum. We had plans to meet in front of the museum. She was late, so I wandered around trying to entertain myself when I came face to face with my next quilt design.

The design on the lamppost looked like an idea for another medallion quilt to me. Studying it, I remembered a picture of a quilted feather pattern that I had in a book at home and wondered if I could manage to fit the design on the lamppost inside the quilted feather pattern. I couldn't wait to get back to the museum with my camera. (But I did have lunch first.)

Using slide film, I photographed the brass design. Projecting my slide on the wall, I moved the projector forward or backward until the projected image was the size that would fit inside the quilted feather pattern. I traced the projected image on paper taped to the wall, and had my pattern! Once again, I didn't plan the whole quilt. Using a 34-inch square piece of unbleached muslin, I appliquéd the lamppost design in the center of it, leaving room on all sides for the feathered quilting which was to be done later. (See Plate 2-15, page 34)

But what to do next? I tried several patchwork designs but liked the stars best. I tried and tried to use a different pattern for the next row of patchwork but still liked the stars and ended up using them twice. But the quilt

Plate 2-11. The St. Louis Art Museum.
Photo: Suzanne Marshall

Plate 2-12. Cass Gilbert's lamppost in front of the St. Louis Art Museum. Photo: Suzanne Marshall

still wasn't big enough. That's when I realized that an appliqué border was needed next. Using leaf and grape patterns from the center, I laid them out on shelf paper next to the stars on the quilt and manipulated them until I felt like they would work for a border. The birds in the corners are from the other side of the lamppost.

Wanting to give credit to the artist who designed the lampposts, I called the art museum library. They said they would research it and call me back. Within a week, I got a call with the information. The architect of the St. Louis Art Museum, Cass Gilbert, had also designed the lampposts, and they had been installed in 1915. The woman who called asked me to bring my quilt to the library for them to see.

I folded the recently finished quilt, put it in a pillow case, and felt very embarrassed going in the art museum with such a bulky package. I had never imagined entering the art museum with a show-and-tell item. My face started to turn a bright pink as the ladies in the library "oohed and aahed" and called others from nearby offices to come see. My face got redder and redder. Suddenly one of the ladies from an adjacent office yelped and ran from the room. In just a few minutes she was back with a beaming face and hand outstretched, holding a slide. For several years, she had been trying to identify the slide of a design in the museum's collection without success. Looking at my quilt, she realized the design was from Cass Gilbert's lampposts outside the art museum and not to be found

Plate 2-13. Closeup of Cass Gilbert's lamppost in front of the St. Louis Museum. PHOTO: GARLAND MARSHALL

Plate 2-14. The other side of Cass Gilbert's lamppost. PHOTO: GARLAND MARSHALL

Plate 2-15. CASS GILBERT REMEMBERED, 89" x 89", 1988.

NEGATIVE COMMENTS

birds in upper corners appear upside down as medallion is directional (Garland loved seeing that comment because he did not like the upside-down birds; if I were to make the quilt again, I would still sew them that way because I wanted the border to be symmetrical, and old Oriental carpets have borders surrounding center designs with the border at the top having upside down design elements, too.)

design elements could be better related (Uh oh, I've heard that before.)

binding too wide (I've heard that before, too.)

would like to have seen some red fabric included in star border (Wow, that certainly would change the quilt.)

POSITIVE COMMENTS

beautiful contrast between colors

richness of colors

graceful

corners good (This judge must not mind upside-down birds.)

good balance

center design well framed by narrow brown fabric (Sorry, it's black.)

border treatment is very effective

very attractive quilt combining together pieced and appliqué

quilting is beautifully executed with nice choice of design

birds are beautiful

what can I say

this is the kind of style and workmanship most quiltmakers try to achieve

in the collection inside the building. The quilt helped her solve the mystery.

I named the quilt *Cass Gilbert Remembered* in honor of the architect. Thanks to *Cass Gilbert Remembered*, I received an all expenses paid trip to the International Quilt Festival in Houston because it was the appliqué grand-prize winner in a contest organized by Better Homes and Gardens Books. It also won awards in Missouri, Indiana, and Vermont and was on the cover of *Quilter's Newsletter Magazine*. Once again, I share the comments made by the judges in all of these competitions.

THOUGHTS FROM GARLAND:

The letter from *Quilter's Newsletter Magazine* asking to use CASS GILBERT REMEMBERED on the cover came at a critical time. Suzanne was in a semiconscious state at the hospital recovering from her bilateral mastectomy. I read her the letter, which was greeted with a big smile, perhaps the first of the week. Over the next hour or so, she asked for me to reread the letter several times as if she were not sure that she hadn't dreamed it.

THOUGHTS FROM GARLAND:

I realize that, if the quilt were on a bed, the birds would all hang right-side up. The quilt, however, was made to be exhibited in the vertical, and I still think the birds should have been turned to a more natural position.

Suzanne is always concerned with giving credit and insecure about using design elements from others. I try to reassure her that it's a common practice for people to be inspired by an artwork and do a variation of that theme or adapt it to another medium. A case in point is the center design from the lamppost. We were visiting the Villa Guilia in Rome, which houses the Etruscan Museum, and there carved in marble was the exact urn with grape leaves. I wonder if Cass Gilbert saw the original marble bas relief, or simply a reproduction, as the basis for his inspiration.

THE OTHER SIDE

Several years later, I needed a small project for a trip we were taking and decided to make a wallhanging out of the design on the other side of Cass Gilbert's lampposts. I appliquéd the birds right side up for Garland.

FRIENDS

A picture from a 1972 UNICEF calendar was my inspiration for entering the Memories of Childhood contest sponsored by the Museum of American Folk Art. My original idea was to show children playing together after supper like we used to do when I was growing up. We played Mother May I, Hide and Seek, jumped rope, and climbed trees. We didn't have televisions and were always eager to run outside to play.

As I was making the quilt, I could see our children on it. When I started the quilt, I didn't know that was going to happen. Our son, Chris, used to love feeding the ducks. Keith used to climb trees wearing his roller skates. Melissa was always eaten alive by insects when she went outdoors, and Lee had a pet snake that got loose all of the time. Notice that Cass Gilbert's squirrel also appears in the quilt.

Friends was the runner-up in Missouri in the Memories of Childhood contest, but was not shown in the exhibit. It was entered in some other competitions without winning prizes.

Plate 2-16. THE OTHER SIDE, 40" x 40", 1992.

Plate 2-17. FRIENDS, 46" x 55", 1988.

NEGATIVE COMMENTS	POSITIVE COMMENTS
quilt tree trunk needs wood-grain quilting	neat "folk" animals (Thanks, Cass Gilbert.)
clothes need quilting	attention to detail is very special
would like to have seen more quilting (Yes, I now agree.)	tiny appliqué with wheels and worms is well done
quilt seems top heavy	excellent workmanship
	you should be proud

Plate 2-18. FULL BLOOM, 73" x 90", 1989. Cass Gilbert's squirrel appears again.

FULL BLOOM

After finishing a quilt, I'm hungry for more. But what to do? I once again looked in Virginia Churchill Bath's book, *Needlework in America*, and found a drawing of an old chain-stitch rug pattern. I read an article in the St. Louis newspaper about a company called Masterlooms unveiling a collection of chain-stitch rugs based on old quilt designs from the Museum of American Folk Art, so why not use a chain-stitch rug design for a quilt?

I'd be much better off if I could imagine an entire quilt in my head or even draw it out on paper before beginning, but that's just too complicated for me. I have to take it one step at a time. So once again, I enlarged the basic rug pattern and then changed several of the flowers on the design. Meanwhile, I added lots of insects, birds, snakes, and even Cass Gilbert's squirrels.

After appliquéing the center, I was faced with figuring out a border. I really liked the zigzag on *Miracles*, so I decided to use that. But, it still wasn't big enough for a complete quilt and, somehow, it didn't look finished. Back to the drawing board! Like *Cass Gilbert Remembered*, I used the leaves and berries from the center of the quilt for an appliqué border, but it was too plain so I added more animals. That was really fun! I searched insect and bird identification guides and looked at children's library books for pictures to simplify, redraw, and adapt to fabric.

Full Bloom became my statement for organic gardening, and it was juried into the Fabric Gardens exhibit, part of the International Garden and Greenery Exposition in Osaka, Japan, in 1990. It won the Silver Award at that show.

SILVER GULL BEACH

My local quilt guild, Circle in the Square, in University City, Missouri, and The Historical Society of University City sponsor the only judged and juried quilt show in the St. Louis area. In 1989, one of the categories for the exhibit was Wall Quilts with Three-Dimensional Surface Treatment. That subject seemed like a pretty good challenge to me, so I started wondering what I could sew with something extra on it.

Looking through my photographs taken during our trip to Australia, I found a picture of silver gulls on the beach on Heron Island. (Plate 2-19) I liked the positions the gulls were in, so I made a slide out of my picture, projected the slide on a piece of paper taped to the wall, and drew around the projected image like I did with Cass Gilbert's lampposts. I had my gull pattern! We've collected seashells through the years, and some aren't perfect and have little holes in them. I sorted through the shells and found some to sew on the quilt. Surely I could add some crabs, too. (Plate 2-19, page 40)

Plate 2-19. Silver gulls on the beach on Heron Island, Australia. Photo: Suzanne Marshall

I didn't tell Garland I was making the quilt and hid it every time he came near my sewing room. My idea was to enter it in the competition with his name on it as the owner, and that would be the first time he'd see the quilt!

Fortunately, the quilt got juried into the competition. I couldn't wait to see what would happen when he found the quilt. Actually, I was doing a pretty risky thing, because at this point, Garland critiques nearly every quilt he sees.

We walked into the exhibit and Garland walked straight to the sea gull quilt. His comment? "Look, Suzanne. This is what you can do with all of your little sea shells!" He did not see his name on it as the owner and walked off to look at the other quilts in the exhibit. Of course, I ended up dragging him back to ask what he really thought about the quilt, and he then looked more closely and discovered that it was his. We later learned that it won first place in its category.

THOUGHTS FROM GARLAND:

This is a particularly favorite story of the quilters who hear Suzanne's lecture. Perhaps they recognize some common quality with the men in their lives. As it is difficult for me to believe that this quilt was constructed under my nose without any suspicion on my part, I must be much more preoccupied and less perceptive than I thought.

Plate 2-20. SILVER GULL BEACH, 47" x 26", 1989.

SCHERENSCHNITTE

A booklet called *Scherenschnitte; Traditional Papercutting* by Claudia Hopf (Applied Arts Publishers, ca. 1977) inspired me to make a quilt. Scherenschnitte is a Swiss-German technique of paper cutting. Three pages in the booklet contain some single-fold designs that were originally intended for Valentines, New Year's greetings, or book plates. These were very intricate designs, but I thought I might be able to enlarge them and redraw some of the edges and inside curves so that I could adapt them to fabric.

I'd heard about freezer paper being useful in appliqué by this time. Although I was satisfied with the needle-turn technique and didn't want any paper in the way, I decided to use the freezer paper to make templates for drawing the pattern on the right side of the fabric to be appliquéd. By having something to iron on the fabric, there wasn't any chance of it slipping while I drew around it. After drawing around the ironed-on freezer-paper template, I removed the freezer paper and basted the appliqué in place on the background. I did not cut the piece out but left it whole until time to appliqué. I learned to cut just ahead of needle-turning to help eliminate fraying fabric.

This was a perfect project to take on a long trip, because the pieces could all be basted on the backgrounds, folded up, and carried along with needle, scissors, and thread in a small sewing bag. I took the squares to New Guinea with us and pulled them out to work on whenever I had the opportunity.

I had no idea what I would do with the finished blocks as I was making them. It wasn't until they were completed and I could start playing with them that I decided to border each of them in the color used for the appliqué and then add the thin red sashing. I felt that gave them some zip. For the border designs, I borrowed elements from the appliquéd Scherenschnitte to try to tie the whole thing together.

Scherenschnitte won the appliqué grand prize from Better Homes and Gardens Books, best workmanship at the Quilter's Heritage Celebration, and first prize in professional appliqué at the AQS show in Paducah, Kentucky.

The best workmanship award has a funny story behind it. When I got ready to put the backing on the quilt, I decided to use the blue fabric, but I didn't have enough. I went back to the store, and unfortunately, they had a new bolt of fabric with a different dye lot. I decided to use it anyway, but to trick the eye, I embroidered a red outline stitch between the binding, which was the original dye lot, and the blue fabric with the

Plate 2-21. Suzanne working on SCHEREN-SCHNITTE, surrounded by New Guinea children, January 1990. PHOTO: GARLAND MARSHALL

Plate 2-22. Embroidery separating the different dye lots on the back of SCHERENSCHNITTE.

Photo: Suzanne Marshall

different dye lot. It must have worked, because the comment I got from the judges in that particular contest was that they loved the embroidery on the back and actually wished that I had put it on the front, too!

NEGATIVE COMMENTS

I can't believe it! I didn't get any negative comments!

POSITIVE COMMENTS

workmanship great and a joy to look at
color adventuresome
wonderful—red really jumps out
love extra touch of stitching on binding
designs wonderful
quilting and appliqué stitches good
well planned—lots of original thought in design

THOUGHTS FROM GARLAND:

As Suzanne mentioned, we enjoy traveling, which is often a fringe benefit of my work as a scientist. Some of her quilts were the result of adapting her techniques so she could take her work with us. I believe blocks of Scherenschnitte were appliquéd in Australia, New Guinea, Italy, and various places in the United States, and on the planes in between.

I didn't realize how recognized some of her quilts were until this past fall. I had been invited to lecture at a meeting in South Africa and received an e-mail message which read:

Dear Professor Marshall:

We don't know you, but do know of your wife. We understand that you will be coming to South Africa. If your wife is accompanying you, we would like to invite her to lecture.

Suzanne and I did go and had a wonderful trip, in no small part due to the hospitality of the quilters during her three lectures (compared with my two lectures).

Plate 2-23. SCHERENSCHNITTE, 78" x 84", 1990.

SIXTIETH WEDDING ANNIVERSARY

Several years after finishing *Scherenschnitte*, I realized that I still had a pattern I hadn't used in the quilt. I made a 60th wedding anniversary present for my parents out of it and hung it in a retrospective show of my quilts the year of their anniversary. The show happened to be in the new Walker Education Center of the Sam Houston Memorial Museum in Huntsville, Texas. My parents discovered it when attending the exhibit.

Plate 2-24. SIXTIETH WEDDING ANNIVERSARY, 43" x 46", 1995.

THOUGHTS FROM GARLAND:

The retrospective show in Huntsville, Texas, was a special event. Suzanne's exhibition inaugurated the new building, which was directly across the street from the house her father had built with his own hands and where she grew up. It was a thrill to see our high school friends as well as friends of both our parents react to the exhibit of 31 of her quilts.

ANNIVERSARY QUILT

Since I saved my *Scherenschnitte* blocks to appliqué only while traveling, I needed an appliqué project to do at home. I cleaned out a drawer one day and came across a greeting card that our four children had given us in 1984, the year that we celebrated our 25th wedding anniversary. I had forgotten all about this card from seven years before, and it definitely sang "quilt" to me when I looked at it again.

I hoped to use two different shades of green for the leaves. I searched every quilt shop in the area, comparing samples of greens, and I couldn't find any greens I liked together. I ended up using black with green highlights, and I think it actually made the quilt more striking.

I used the same method for making this quilt that I used for *Miracles*, *Cass Gilbert Remembered*, and *Full Bloom* by appliquéing the center before I had an inkling of an idea what would happen next. That got me in a bit of trouble because I ran out of the background fabric when I started adding borders and ended up with a different dye lot again. I felt like it wouldn't be that noticeable, so used it and forgot about it.

One thing leads to another, or one border tells me what to do next. There are certainly plenty of disadvantages to this method, but the exciting part is that the quilt is always a surprise to me when it's finished because it turns into something I've never imagined in the beginning.

Anniversary Quilt has been good to me, and for the third straight year, it won the appliqué grand prize from Better Homes and Gardens Books. They retired me from the contest! The quilt also won best of show at the Missouri State Fair, the Vermont Quilt Festival, and the Dogwood Festival in Tennessee. But the quilt didn't even get juried into the AQS show in Paducah, and it received some negative comments from some other competitions, where it won prizes anyway (comments on page 47).

THOUGHTS FROM GARLAND:

I refer to this quilt as the "Paducah reject" and feel it teaches a valuable lesson. As I remind Suzanne when she gets back her judges' comments, "every quilt has its judges, you just have to find them!" At the level of competition seen at the major quilt shows, most, if not all, of the quilts are technically superb and have stunning designs with excellent color and fabric selection. The judges must, in the final analysis, be swayed by their own preferences in style to make a final decision. Certainly, I seldom agree with the choice for best of show. But then, I have my own favorite quilters, one of whose quilts would probably get my vote. Only by entering a quilt in several shows and getting comments from several different judges do you get a realistic assessment of its merits.

Plate 2-25. ANNIVERSARY QUILT. Closeup of embroidery on birds.

Plate 2-26. ANNIVERSARY QUILT, 79" x 93", 1991.

NEGATIVE COMMENTS

some threads showing on appliqué (It did win best of show in that competition anyway.)

two gray fabrics used—not consistent placement! (I had completely forgotten about the different dye lots until I read that.)

two knots found on back

POSITIVE COMMENTS

magnificent balance of design and color

outstanding appliqué

beautiful binding front and back with nice embroidery addition to binding (I used the Scherenschnitte embroidery trick.)

no ripples

beautifully appliquéd border

vibrant, beautiful quilt

black touches add zest!

fabulous color choices throughout

piecing well-handled

embroidery stitches add a nice touch

I like this quilt

JOURNEY THROUGH TIME

I'm always on the lookout for quilt designs—architectural details, mosaic floor tiles, rug patterns, greeting cards, photographs, you name it. But this time I found a small black and white picture of an early 17th-century embroidery piece with motifs from herbals, samplers, and pattern books of the day, recalling the ancient Tree of Life. I later learned that it lives at the Metropolitan Art Museum in New York City. Looking at the small picture (about five inches square), I wondered if I could transform it to a large piece of appliqué. I couldn't distinguish everything on it, and thought some complicated flowers instead of large globular fruits might make it more interesting, so I enlarged the embroidery and started adding design elements of my own.

I put the background together, decided on the tree fabric, and began. I didn't plan what colors I would use before beginning, just started appliquéing, starting in the center and going out toward the edges. I was pretty discouraged, because I didn't feel like it was working together. It was a snowy, icy January when I started working on this quilt, and I "hibernated" and sewed. Garland would come home from work each day and say, "What did you sew on today?" I'd say, "One butterfly and this flower, but it's just not looking right with all of these different colors." Garland would say, "Just keep going." That kind of conversation went on day after day. I have to give Garland credit—he kept cheering me on and wouldn't let me quit. It wasn't until the border was on that I felt like the whole thing came together. After I finished, I discovered I had used nearly 150 different fabrics in the quilt.

While appliquéing the clouds, I noticed they were receding in the background fabric because the colors were too similar. I decided to outline the clouds with embroidery and also used that technique around some of the animals that weren't standing out of the background enough.

Plate 2-27. Detail of embroidery on JOURNEY THROUGH TIME.

The design motifs under the fish in the small drawing were indistinguishable, so I added little critters that I liked. I started wondering what the original embroidery looked like. How large was it? What colors were used?

After I finished appliquéing the top and was busy with the quilting, we planned a trip to New York City. I made an appointment with the Curator of European Textiles at the Metropolitan Art Museum, hoping she would allow us to see the 17th-century embroidery. She kindly took us behind lock and key in the storage area of the museum and brought out the original embroidery for us to see. What an exciting moment! The original embroidery is only about 24" x 21" in size and is very muted in color. We were told that it was probably faded and a better idea of the original color could be known if the embroidery were

Plate 2-28. EMBROIDERED FRUITING TREE, 23¾" x 21¼", English, first half of the 17th century. Photo Courtesy of the Metropolitan Museum of Art, Gift of Irwin Untermyer, 1964. (64.101.1305)

Plate 2-29. JOURNEY THROUGH TIME, 68" x 68", 1991.

NEGATIVE COMMENTS

border piecing could be improved; some
points don't exactly meet on the border
binding doesn't feel like the batting is even
quilting in appliqué areas is better than borders; stitches should be even

POSITIVE COMMENTS

impressed with appliqué technique
fantastic work with fabrics
like outline of appliqué with embroidery
delightful attention to detail

taken out of the frame and turned over to see the back where the colors hadn't been exposed to light.

The reason we couldn't distinguish what was underneath the fish in the small drawing was because there was a woven braid all around the edge of the frame. The braid partially covered and shadowed the edges of the embroidery. Peeking behind the braid, I could see what had been embroidered there. Lo and behold, there was a grasshopper embroidered underneath the same fish where I had appliquéd a grasshopper.

Garland said, "I know what *you* were doing five lifetimes ago!"

Journey Through Time has also been good to me. It won a major prize in Holland at Quilt Expo Europa III and was on the cover of *Quilter's Newsletter Magazine*. It also won the top prize in the Columbus Heritage Quilt Show in Columbus, Indiana, an incredible prize of $2,500. But even though I won that top prize, I received negative criticisms, which I share along with the positive ones (page 49).

THOUGHTS FROM GARLAND:

Quilting has expanded both our horizons. Certainly, seeing the original embroidery and realizing the emotional connection between Suzanne and the woman who had embroidered the piece some centuries before was a highlight. We were able to attend the show in the Hague as it coincided with a meeting in Italy that I was attending. I volunteered as a "white-glove person" and tried to explain Caryl Bryer Fallert's method of constructing her quilt to the large, enthusiastic crowds.

Actually, the judges were right. The batting that Suzanne used separated on the edges during quilting and she had tried to repair it, but it must have been obvious upon feeling the quilt. It certainly wasn't apparent upon viewing it.

BED BUGS

After finishing *Scherenschnitte* in 1990, I knew I needed another quilt to work on while traveling. It was essential to come up with a design that could be basted on the background and then pulled out during airplane rides and in hotel rooms. Garland had agreed to be a visiting professor in Florence, Italy, which also included lectures in about six other Italian cities. I knew I would have lots of time alone in strange places and hotel rooms. I'm pretty good about exploring places by myself (and searching for new quilt designs), but I knew I couldn't keep that up all day without wearing myself out.

On a previous trip to Italy, we visited Piazza Armerina in Sicily, which arose in its present site in the 12th century. This special place is famous for the third- to fifth-century Roman Villa of Casale, which contains splendid mosaic pavements. I bought postcards there, always an inspiration to me when planning a new quilt. Among the mosaic-floored corridors were medallions of wreaths composed of leaves and containing heads of animals in the middle. That gave me the idea to design a wreath that could be basted on the background, later adding something (at that time I had no idea what) in the middle of the wreaths. (Plate 2-30)

I left just enough space between the

leaves so the basted leaves did not overlap. Finishing one wreath, I realized that they were too plain, so I added the berries. I still didn't know what to put in the middle.

The wreaths kept me very busy in Italy and on other subsequent trips as well, but as I neared completion of the 16 wreaths, I started searching my mind for something I could arrange in the middle. Our trip to New Guinea to collect moths with an entomologist came back to me. We had become fascinated with the bugs while we were there—such vivid colors and incredible shapes and sizes. We bought a *Handbook of Common New Guinea Beetles* and actually collected a few beetles (dead and preserved) to bring back with us. I had my answer!

What fun to start arranging bugs backed into each other to make kaleidoscope designs in the center! I didn't like using the bug shapes by themselves, because the design looked square in a round wreath. That's why I ended up adding flowers between the bugs to round out the design. But, of course, I hadn't dreamed up any of this before I started, and I ended up with another complete surprise when I finished.

I remember showing a completed block at my quilt guild meeting and was later told by a friend that one of the members turned up her nose and said, "Who would put *bugs* inside a Christmas wreath?" Of course, I didn't know that I was making a Christmas wreath. (Plate 2-31)

The bugs crawling around the border can be used to play a game. Every bug inside a wreath can be found twice on the borders in different colors. Can you find them? (Plate 2-32, page 52)

I hoped that people looking at the quilt at an exhibit would see it as a traditional-looking quilt from a distance and then be surprised by finding the unexpected bugs upon closer inspection. And it worked! What fun for me to watch people casually stroll by the quilt and then start laughing after discovering the bugs. I've heard several people say, "I certainly wouldn't want to *sleep* under it!"

Bed Bugs has won first place awards at the International Quilt Festival in Houston

Plate 2-30. Piazza Armerina wreath. PHOTO: SUZANNE MARSHALL

Plate 2-31. Stipple quilting fills in the design made by the bugs.

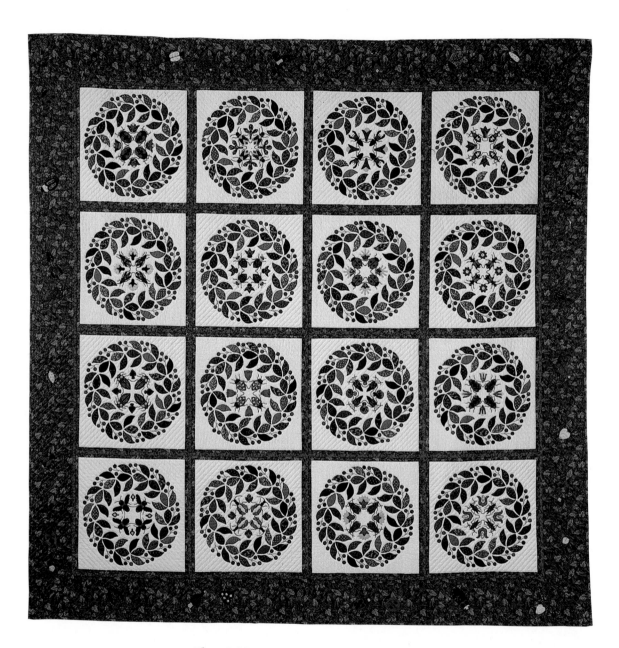

Plate 2-32. BED BUGS, 92" x 92", 1992.

TAKE-AWAY APPLIQUÉ

(as well as viewer's choice); Rockome Gardens; Silver Dollar City; and University City, Missouri. Second place awards were won at the American Quilter's Society show, and Quilter's Heritage Celebration. *Bed Bugs* and *Miracles* were both invited to be part of Past and Present: Ongoing Traditions in American Craft Art to celebrate The Year of American Craft in 1993 at the Mitchell Museum in Mount Vernon, Illinois, and the Evansville Museum of Art and Science in Evansville, Indiana.

THOUGHTS FROM GARLAND:

Bed Bugs makes people smile. It was selected viewer's choice at the International Quilt Festival in Houston. Good humor always has an element of surprise, and the quilt evolved as a visual joke. Besides, insects are diverse in form, often incredibly beautiful and historically of artistic significance. An example would be the common use of the scarab beetle in Egyptian art and jewelry.

NEGATIVE COMMENTS
    miters off on 2 corners—otherwise wonderful

POSITIVE COMMENTS
    outstanding design and workmanship
    lovely embroidery
    wonderful design concept
    like stippling
    wow—your quilt really dynamic; I love it
    imaginative use of insects and wreaths
    quilt lays very flat and even
    red inset border sets off entire quilt!
    the closer you get the more you see and enjoy
        (Oh, goodie! That's what I hoped.)
    bugs are incredible
    a wonderful example of how every quilt should
        be! (Does that ever make me feel good!)

THE MASTECTOMY

About this time, I got the urge to try making something non-traditional. I wondered if I could get juried into Quilt National and knew that nothing I'd previously made would be considered, much less accepted. Having time in Italy while Garland was a visiting professor gave me a bit more time to think about a completely different project.

Since my bilateral mastectomy in 1989, I am alarmed when I hear stories about women who have found lumps in their breasts but have not sought treatment because of an overwhelming fear of disfigurement. Perhaps my non-traditional quilt could send a message—a changed body is not what is important. Life is!

I also wanted to stimulate conversation about a topic not discussed very much. Maybe if women would talk about breast cancer, it might not be as scary. In addition, I have a concern that many women do not realize they have a real choice regarding implants or cosmetic surgery. It is not necessary to conform to society's image.

While these thoughts were bubbling around in my head and trying to take form, we visited the Monastery of Monte Oliveto Maggiore near Siena. On the walls of this large cloister are 15th-century frescoes painted by Signorelli and Sodoma, depicting the life of St. Benedict and showing scenes in different time frames within the same picture. I began wondering about how I could make a narrative quilt expressing my concerns connected with my own experience. I'm not an "artist" when it comes to drawing figures, so how could I say what I wanted to say, since I needed to use people? We visited the *enoteca*, or wine cellar, in Montalcino and there was my answer! There was a "modern art" mural on the wall with extremely simplified figures. Perhaps I could do it after all.

My first step was to draw in a tiny notepad the simple figures depicting what I wanted them to say. When I got home, I made pattern pieces for the figures and moved them around on the floor to try to come up with a format. Garland came home from work each day saying, "Are you still playing with paper dolls?" (Plate 2-33)

When I finally got the format I wanted, I drew around the figures on a big piece of paper and then drew the puzzle shapes around them. Before I started sewing the quilt, I asked our sons if it would embarrass them. They said, "Mom, you have to make this quilt!" They pointed out that women's health issues are of national interest and the dangers of breast implants are something to be concerned about. I had to keep going!

The narrative for the quilt reads from left to right. The first piece (upper left) depicts a healthy, whole woman walking along with everything okay in her world. Then she gets

Plate 2-33. Trying to decide on a format for THE MASTECTOMY quilt. Photo: Suzanne Marshall

a mammogram (lower left). The red piece at the top registers shock and denial at the diagnosis. Surgery follows. Below, there's a trash can: "Throw them out!" And the big C, cancer, is scary! And to the right, the puzzle piece with the patient in her hospital gown shows the stitches where she had the mastectomy. Finally, she goes back to the doctor, who asks her if she would like to have more surgery for implants. She says, "NO!" The message of the quilt (lower right) portrays the figure with a changed body but definitely enjoying life amidst flowers and music.

I had a great time making the quilt. I tried sewing with metallic thread for the first time (her surgical stitches) and even came up with something plastic to sew on the quilt for the implants (we now have a hole in our shower curtain!).

It has been fascinating to watch people view the quilt. It has evoked strong emotions, a few tears, some disgust, and has served as a catalyst for conversation. Many women share stories about loved ones going through the experience or who have died from breast cancer. I have watched men study the quilt and come back to stand in front of it silently several more times.

The quilt can be interpreted in different ways depending on the viewer, and that's just fine with me. I've heard many interpretations for the heads above the operating table: doctors and nurses, the staff discussing the treatment, her emotions, imaging cancer cells out of her body, all of her family and friends trying to figure out how to help, all of the women in the past who have had breast cancer, or all of those people who try to tell you what to do when something goes wrong.

The quilt did not get juried into Quilt National, but did get accepted as part of the

Plate 2-34. THE MASTECTOMY, 64" x 52", 1992.

PHOTO: RED ELF

COMMENTS:

What I like about this quilt is I feel I know or understand the pain suffered by the maker. The imagery is original and so personal—the subtle jigsaw puzzle background adds to the impact. Color is where I see a slight need for improvement.

Other comments from exhibits include: appreciate personal statement; conveys theme well; quilting motifs enrich.

Healing Legacies exhibit, which was shown for the first time in the rotunda of the House of Representatives in Washington, D.C. It was later exhibited in the Missouri State Capitol Building and the New England Quilt Museum. It has been invited to be part of cancer awareness programs and exhibits in hospitals, including the Misericordia Hospital in Edmonton, Alberta. *The Mastectomy* also won an award of excellence for art quilt at the International Quilt Festival in Houston, Texas.

TOUJOURS NOUVEAU

Garland loves art nouveau, the art movement popular around the turn of the century. Emphasizing forms derived from nature, art nouveau was characterized by fluid movement and a lack of straight lines. I started looking in every art nouveau book I could find for design ideas, wanting to make a special quilt for Garland. I found a book published by Dover with copyright-free drawings called *Art Nouveau Designs* by Ed Sibbett, Jr. In the book are four pen and ink type drawings that caught my eye. Perhaps, with a bit of modification, I could adjust the designs and make them suit-

able for fabric.

For this quilt, I wanted to use softer, more subdued colors that were still strong enough to "sing." Since I've never enjoyed pastel colors, finding just the right fabrics was a major challenge for me. I started this quilt the same way I started the others—one panel at a time and without having any notion about how the end result would look. I couldn't even think about how the whole thing would go together until the fourth panel was completed.

The panels were the most difficult appliqué I have ever done because of the ribbons. Each panel has different-colored ribbons composed of three different shades of fabric in the same color range. The colors had to change as the ribbons twisted. I couldn't figure out what to sew on first and then second and third. I figured if I could sew on just one thing, maybe that would tell me what went on next. And that's what happened. I started, kept going, and had faith that it would somehow become a quilt.

Shortly after I finished *Toujours Nouveau*, I entered it in the AQS show. It won the Gingher Award for Hand Workmanship. I was stunned! That meant $10,000, but it also meant losing the quilt because it would

THOUGHTS FROM GARLAND:

Many people assume that Suzanne used *The Mastectomy* quilt as therapy for dealing with her surgery. In my opinion, both she and her psyche had fully recovered when she began this project. Because of her increased sensitivity to the impact of society on women's image, or even discussing breast cancer, she felt she had a story to tell. This was very courageous for her because of her highly developed sense of privacy and general resistance to personal exposure, but she felt the topic was significant. I was also impressed with the intensity of her creative experience. She worked almost continuously once the design was completed. I have been amazed at how this quilt has stimulated women to discuss their own fears and experiences. Many times I have watched women look at this quilt with tears running down their cheeks.

Plate 2-35. TOUJOURS NOUVEAU, 68" x 80", 1993.

PHOTO: RICHARD WALKER

become part of the collection of the Museum of the American Quilter's Society. This same year, Jonathan Shannon's quilt *Airshow* won best of show, and we had a long discussion about whether to give up our "children."

Garland and I agonized over what to do, and after visiting the beautiful museum, we decided that it would be a wonderful place for the quilt to live. We have visited it there several times.

THOUGHTS FROM GARLAND:

When the quilt top was nearly finished, I suggested that there were not enough grapes appliquéd on one of the panels. Suzanne ignored my comment several times, but finally said that, if I wanted more grapes, I knew where the purple fabric was. I decided to call her bluff and selected several fabrics, cut out the circles and placed them where I thought they would be most effective. In any case, she appliquéd them in place. I related this story to a friend while standing with Suzanne in front of the quilt at the AQS show. The next day, I overheard a quilter say to a friend near the exhibit, "Did you know that her husband selected the fabrics and cut out all the pieces for her?"

Another memorable image is that of a group of English quilters on their way to the AQS show who had been visiting Suzanne at our home when she was called and notified of her prize. They would come and check on her and the quilt at the show on a regular basis, almost as if the event was a scheduled part of their tour.

It was a difficult but correct decision to give up my quilt, but everyone won. The AQS museum got the quilt and have displayed it in an ideal setting, Suzanne got the check for the prize of $10,000, and the IRS got a check from me for the income tax.

ADAM AND EVE

Searching through more library books, I found a small black and white drawing of another 17th-century embroidery. This one was of Adam and Eve. I read that the embroidery had been adapted from a frontispiece in a Bible made in the 16th century and that it was thought that the Bible frontispiece had been adapted from a Venetian drawing from the 15th century. Design elements and motifs changed throughout the centuries, but some stayed the same. It seemed like perfect appliqué material.

Once again, I enlarged the drawing and then changed several of the animals and birds on it. The original embroidery was only 8¾" x 13½", and I would guess that the Bible frontispiece was probably not much larger than that. My appliqué would surely look quite different, but I did want the positions of the camels and elephants to stay the same through all of those translations in different art forms.

Borrowing designs from other sources made me feel guilty in the beginning, but I now feel that it is a wonderful way to keep these designs alive through history. They evolve and change, yet the original essence of the design comes through each work. Other words for "evolve"—such as develop, grow, emerge—seem to illustrate what has happened to Adam and Eve through the centuries.

Not only does the *Adam and Eve* quilt connect me with the past, it also connects me with people and events in the present. Christmas Eve of 1992 comes to mind. Our daughter, Melissa, was expecting her first baby. That morning, all of my thoughts were directed her way. The phone rang that Christmas Eve at the very moment that I was embroidering around Eve on my *Adam and Eve* quilt. It was our daughter telling us our granddaughter had just been born. Since she had the baby at home with a midwife, the call was made mere minutes after her birth. Now, how can I look at that quilt without thinking about Sasha, our granddaughter? The quilt will be hers.

The quilt was in an invitational exhibit at the Museum of the American Quilter's Society, but I have entered it in only one competition. It did not win anything, but the comments were positive: lovely folk art piece; black line embroidery really enhances it.

Plate 2-36. ADAM AND EVE, 68" x 49", 1993.

Plate 2-37. DRAGONFLOWERS, 82" x 82", 1994.

DRAGONFLOWERS

Selecting fabric for quilts is one of the joys of life. It's hard to resist the many nuances of color and implied texture. I used to collect quarter-yard pieces of fabric, but with Garland's encouragement, have gone to half-yard pieces when buying something I "might" use someday. After all, how can a painter paint without paints, and how can a quilter quilt without fabrics?

Over the years, I've collected some colors that I rarely use. Purple is one of those colors. I love looking at it on the bolt but have no idea what to do with it in a quilt. I decided to challenge myself to make a purple quilt and thought I'd better try to appliqué another art nouveau design since Garland lost his quilt to the museum.

Art Nouveau Floral Iron-On Transfer Patterns by Ed Sibbett, Jr., a Dover book with small patterns, has a picture on the front that looked suitable to adapt for appliqué. And I could make the flowers purple. I did the center appliqué and it looked totally dead. I thought I was using fairly bright colors, but they weren't singing to me. I thought maybe it was because I didn't really like the color purple. I tried using some golds with it, but that didn't work either. After several other color experiments I found a piece of mottled orange, red, and purple fabric that seemed to make the purple come alive. I used different parts of that one piece of fabric for the flower centers.

For the borders I tried opening up the center design so that it could be surrounded with similar leaves and flowers. The black art nouveau scroll was drawn to cover my seam lines between the center and large flower border.

I found an interesting idea for the background quilting in a book called *Tilings and Patterns* by Branko Grunbaum and G.C. Shephard, (W.H. Freeman and Company, c. 1987). This is really a book for mathematicians and scientists, but I try to overlook that and just look at the pictures. The tiling is taken from a 16th-century Persian drawing in the British Museum. (Fig. 2-2, page 63)

A little 6-year-old boy named the quilt. He came to a retrospective exhibit of my quilts with his school class, and I was demonstrating quilting on the "purple" quilt. He asked what I was going to name it, and I said I didn't know, did he have any ideas? He said, "Well, it has dragonflies on it, and it has flowers on it. Why don't you name it *Dragonflowers*?" So I did!

Dragonflowers has won prizes in several states and has received judges' critiques.

NEGATIVE COMMENTS
quilting stitches should be consistent in size

POSITIVE COMMENTS
quilting stitch well done
a bold statement
good use of black
excellent choice of quilting designs
dynamic quilt
good design and color—very effective
like embroidery in binding; binding well
applied
nice flowing design
good fabric choices
best features are detail inside binding, appliqué,
and appliqué design in inner and outer border
well balanced design—motion created
color choice exciting
appliqué technique excellent

Plate 2-38. The Quilts Cure retrospective exhibit to raise money for pediatric cancer research, Plaza Frontenac, St. Louis, March, 1994. Photo: Garland Marshall

THOUGHTS FROM GARLAND:

A very special retrospective exhibit in our hometown of St. Louis was held to raise money for pediatric cancer research at St. Louis Children's Hospital, part of the Washington University Medical School complex. A close friend, Marnie Hauff, whose son had died of leukemia, was responsible for conceiving and organizing the event. For several weeks, Suzanne spent the afternoon at the show, demonstrating quilting without a hoop or a frame and interacting with the visitors. The exhibit was a huge success, raising over $53,000 after all the expenses were paid, and it exposed many people in the area to contemporary quilting and Suzanne's work, including several neighbors who were not aware of her talents.

One of my graduate students took pictures at the retrospective show, and Suzanne gave him some of her note cards. I was sitting in my office when her quilts suddenly started appearing on my computer screen. The student had scanned the images on the cards and inserted them into my screen-saver program, which alternates images when my computer is idle. This was some surprise for me and started a series of events which resulted in Suzanne's home page (http://www.ibc.wustl.edu/quilts/srm.htm), which focuses on her quilts being on the Internet (again initially created as a surprise by my students). This has provided a convenient means for some to discover her quilts.

Fig. 2-2. Background quilting tiling pattern.

THOUGHTS FROM GARLAND:

Lucky again! The Quilt Expo in Lyon, France, was held the weekend before a meeting on Capri to which I had been invited, so we had an excuse to attend the quilt show. The exhibit was packed, and the convention center not sufficiently large to handle the crowds. At one point, the doors had to be closed, and one glass door was accidentally broken. The resulting crash caused one woman to think it was a terrorist attack and she threw herself to the floor. Police were called to control the "quilt riot" according to the Houston paper. Fortunately, no one was hurt, and the show was a great success.

As a special aspect of these shows, quilters from different European countries make group presentations. The increased attendance over previous years and rapid improvement in the quilts shown indicates how popular quilting is becoming in Europe. There were several opportunities for Suzanne to meet the other contestants from around the world, whose quilts were simply spectacular.

RHAPSODY IN BLOOM

I've enjoyed working with art nouveau designs because of the graceful, flowing lines and interpretation of floral forms. Searching many books with art nouveau themes to help me, I drew out the nine patterns for *Rhapsody In Bloom*, adapting portions of flowers and leaves from an assortment of pictures.

Rhapsody In Bloom was juried in the Artistic Expressions competition sponsored by *Quilter's Newsletter Magazine* in conjunction with Quilt Expo V in Lyon, France. It won an honorable mention in workmanship, and at the time of this writing, has been away from home for a year now.

Plate 2-39. Detail from RHAPSODY IN BLOOM.

Plate 2-40. RHAPSODY IN BLOOM, 76" x 86", 1996.

DON'T BUG ME!

*B*ed Bugs was such a fun quilt to make. I found myself looking for "bug" fabric in stores, and knew that I needed to make another bug quilt. I had collected some antique gold fabrics that I wanted to use as a challenge to work with different colors. Since I had just finished the very bright *Rhapsody in Bloom*. I wanted to make a more subdued quilt and selected fabrics to go with the antique golds.

I hoped to make kaleidoscope designs with flowers and bugs. Since they were round designs and I wanted to put them in a square format, I drew the gold borders to put in the corners of the squares to fill out the rounded centers. I had lots of fun playing with bug and flower shapes to make designs, and I drew out 16 patterns before I realized I'd made so many.

When I finished the appliqué on the first square, Garland saw it and immediately stuck up his nose because of the colors. He apparently does not like antique gold. He spent no time letting his view be known. He really wanted me to use bright colors. I thought about it but decided to keep going. Maybe I'd just make four squares for a wallhanging if he really didn't like it. I finished the four squares. He kept telling me he didn't like the colors. I thought, "Well, I have all of these patterns drawn out—maybe I'll make nine squares instead of four for a wallhanging." Finishing those, I knew I had to keep going.

Now here's the funny part. While I was appliquéing the squares and Garland was fussing about the color, he went to the store and bought two neckties. It wasn't until he got home that he realized that the main colors in the ties were antique gold and black.

I named the quilt *Don't Bug Me!* because that's what I felt like saying to Garland as he kept trying to persuade me to change the color scheme.

In its first competition, *Don't Bug Me!* did not win a prize. I thought, "Who knows? Maybe Garland's right!" Later the quilt won prizes at the Quilter's Heritage Celebration and the AQS Show and the best of show at a local show in St. Louis, Missouri. When I was informed about the best of show prize, I responded, "You're kidding! I didn't expect to win anything!" The reply was, "Well, of course it's certainly not one of MY favorite quilts!" I was reminded once again that, not only do judges disagree, viewers often do not agree with the judges.

THOUGHTS FROM GARLAND:
    Suzanne asks my opinion and I give it. She then decides whether it was what she wanted to hear and does what she wanted to anyway. Occasionally, she finds some value in my comments, which is fine. If I were going to spend several months on a quilt, I certainly wouldn't have chosen this color scheme. With regard to the ties, I plead guilty. Just living with the quilt blocks must have influenced me.

Plate 2-41. DON'T BUG ME, 82" x 82", 1996.

NEGATIVE COMMENTS

shadow of seam allowances

with so much happening in this quilt, it seems a bit busy

POSITIVE COMMENTS

bugs—for something that I don't care for that much, this is a wonderful quilt

delightful, charming quilt

design is great and unusual

beautiful work

creative

artistically rendered

whimsical quality

fabric choices one of the best features

what a fun quilt

all elements working well, innovative design and impeccable craftsmanship

Congratulations!!

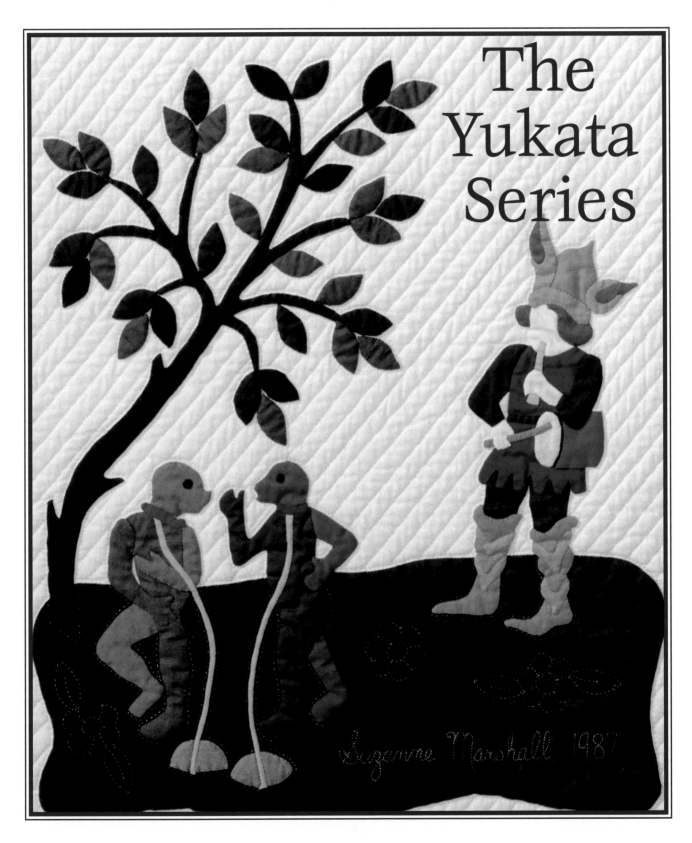

The Yukata Series

In 1972, our family met a delightful Japanese couple, Akira and Akemi Konishi, who were living in St. Louis for a couple of years. We became friends, and when they returned to Japan, we missed them. We corresponded over the years, and when we made a visit to Japan in 1984, we visited with them and renewed our friendship. Akemi learned that I was interested in making patchwork quilts, and she knew that I would appreciate the beautiful Japanese cotton yukata fabrics that she had been saving through the years. She gave me many of the yukata fabric samples to bring home and use for quiltmaking. They were about 10" x 14" in size and had holes in parts of them where they had been attached to sample books. I was thrilled with the gift and spent many hours gazing at the patterns and deciding what to make.

JAPANESE FANS

Fans seemed like a good pattern to use to convey the Japanese spirit reflected in yukata fabrics. Unfortunately, I was disappointed with the quilt after I pieced it and must admit that I never finished the quilting. I was sorry I had cut the fabric into such small pieces. The essence of the exquisite patterns on the fabrics was lost by using such small pieces.

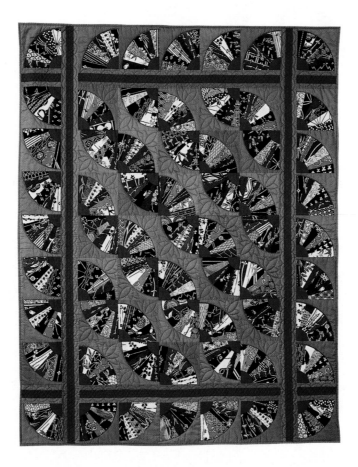

Plate 3-1. JAPANESE FANS, 66" x 86", 1990.

AKEMI KONISHI

What could I do to use larger pieces of cloth so that more of the motif on the fabrics showed? An Evening Star block that is 8" square has a 4" square in the middle. That would certainly use larger pieces of fabric and feature the special Japanese motifs a bit better. I started sewing Evening Stars right away and enjoyed using a clear plastic template so I could see to select the part of the fabric to feature in the block. The quilt was named for my friend, Akemi Konishi.

The quilt won a first prize in a local competition and received the comments from the judges, shown below.

Plate 3-2. AKEMI KONISHI, 89" x 98", 1991.

POSITIVE COMMENTS
    creative use of Japanese fabrics
    color is limited but very handsome both backing
      and border

well-planned scrap quilt
nice choice for backing
you should be quite proud of this

THOUGHTS FROM GARLAND:
    At Suzanne's retrospective show in Peoria, Illinois, she was approached by a woman, who asked if the quilt was named after a Japanese woman living in Kyoto. When Suzanne replied yes, the woman told how she had been lost in Kyoto and rescued by Akemi, who had taken her to get some tea and had given her some fabric. I took a picture of the woman and Suzanne in front of the quilt, named in honor of Akemi, and sent the photo to her. At a different exhibit, another woman told Suzanne that she had worked with Akemi in Japan in 1976. It is truly a small world, and special people like Akemi make a strong impression.

KONNICHIWA

Some of the fabrics that Akemi gave to me had geometrical motifs on them, possibly used for men's summer kimonos. Once again, I searched the pattern books to find a traditional block that would feature the fabrics. The World's Fair block has a 4¼" square in the middle. The third Japanese quilt, named *Konnichiwa*, which means "good afternoon" in Japanese, features different geometrical motif fabrics in each of the 42 blocks.

Konnichiwa received a best of show award at the Rockome Gardens Quilt Celebration in Illinois and received some positive comments from the judges (on this page).

AKIRA KONISHI

In the collection of Japanese fabrics were some that contained white backgrounds with blue in the pattern. I hoped for more than a 4" square to feature these fabrics. Searching the pattern books once again, I found the traditional pattern called King David's Crown. A 12½" block has a 5" block in the center. This allowed even larger pieces of the special fabrics to be highlighted in the quilt named *Akira Konishi*. (Plate 3-4, page 72)

Surrounding the blue-on-white fabrics with some of the scraps from *Konnichiwa* added to the design, but I didn't like the two right next to each other without a bit of red. Therefore, I embroidered the outline stitch between the two fabrics.

Adding a bit of appliqué where the squares join one another adds another dimension to *Akira Konishi*. (Fig. 3-1, page 73)

Akira Konishi has also won a few prizes around the country. The judges apparently really felt like writing about this one, see comments page 73.

THOUGHTS FROM GARLAND:
    Actually, I wanted to name the quilt "Konishi wa," which means "the Konishis are the topic," but we were afraid of embarrassing our Japanese friends with all the attention. Since the original title sounded so much like konnichiwa, a common Japanese expression, we decided to use that instead.

POSITIVE COMMENTS
  excellent workmanship
  quilting is visually exciting
  nice use of Japanese fabrics with U.S. fabrics
  excellent small sashing strips finely pieced

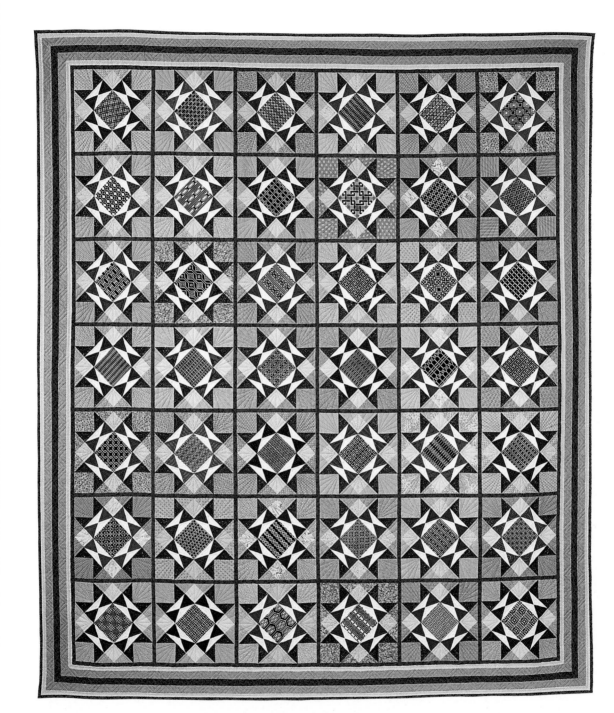

Plate 3-3. KONNICHIWA, 89" x 98", 1992.

Plate 3-4. AKIRA KONISHI, 72" x 89", 1995.

NEGATIVE COMMENTS

too balanced for Oriental work theme, I believe

assorted grays in background area with more lights would be helpful

more value change would be appreciated—lighter areas needed (Were they really looking at Akira Konishi when they wrote that?)

border treatment less imaginative than the rest

straight line piecing should be straight (See first positive comment.)

POSITIVE COMMENTS

excellent precision of workmanship (So who's right?)

lovely piecing—fabrics are great; beautifully executed piece

stunning quilt

beautifully planned and put together

you've combined Japanese fabrics with regular quilt fabrics and brought out the best in each

original, wonderful

excellent use of yukata fabrics

special attention to detail, gives your quilt a wonderful quality; love how you appliquéd the center of the stars; your choice of quilting really enhanced the Japanese fabrics

crisp and pleasing design

innovative use of this smashing fabric

red stitching around blocks a great touch

elements work well together

nice use of extensive fabric collection

Fig. 3-1. Appliqué motif for AKIRA KONISHI.

ARIGATO

By now, most of the fabric samples that Akemi gave me were in fairly small pieces. I couldn't search for another traditional pattern with large squares, but still wanted to find something that would feature all of the fabrics. Star of Hope, by Marcia Aasmundstad, 1980, was my choice. Once again, a touch of appliqué adds some complexity to a simple block.

Arigato won a prize in a local quilt show in St. Louis, Missouri.

The quilt's name, *Arigato,* means "thank you" in Japanese.

NEGATIVE COMMENTS
   quilt needs to be calmed down; perhaps making the outside pieces of the border blocks dark would have done that
   some of interior red strips distort somewhat at seam intersections

POSITIVE COMMENTS
   overall, great
   fabric choices interesting
   beautiful work!!!

Fig. 3-2. Appliqué motif for ARIGATO.

Plate 3-5. ARIGATO, 72" x 80½", 1997.

TACUINUM SANITATIS, NATURAL HISTORY MAGAZINE. COURTESY OF THE SPENCER COLLECTION, THE NEW YORK PUBLIC LIBRARY, ASTOR, LENOX AND TILDEN FOUNDATION.

Lap Quilting

I would probably never have started quilting if I thought I had to use a big quilting frame. We didn't have room for one, and I like to move around from room to room when I quilt.

I decided I'd just baste the layers together and see if I could fill in with the quilting. I found that I needed lots of basting, but that's okay, it just takes a bit longer and makes it much easier in the long run.

Here's how I baste a quilt to get ready for the quilting:

First, pin the backing of the quilt all around the edges to a tightly woven carpet. A shag rug or carpet with long loops won't work. The carpet needs to be similar to an indoor-outdoor or tightly woven berber type carpet. While pinning the backing, stretch it so that it looks tight. The pins are pushed through the edges of the backing straight into the carpet and pad. (Plate 4-1)

Next, pat the batt down on the backing, smoothing out any wrinkles. Do not stretch the batt. (Plate 4-2)

Now for the top. Stretch the top the same amount that you stretched the backing and pin it through the batt, backing, carpet, and pad all around the edges. Line up any lattice strips or straight edges while pinning. It is sometimes necessary to go around the quilt twice, adjusting the pins so that the quilt is straight and it looks evenly tight. (Plate 4-3)

Turn on your favorite music or radio station. Sit in the middle of the quilt (it's not going anywhere, because it is being held tightly around the edges) and start basting. The direction of the basting stitches does not matter. You can make diagonal lines from corner to corner (this is what I usually do first) and then make horizontals, verticals, and lots of curves and circles. As the music

Plate 4-1. Pinning backing to carpet. PHOTO: GARLAND MARSHALL

Plate 4-2. Placing batt on backing. PHOTO: GARLAND MARSHALL

Plate 4-3. Pinning the top to the batt and backing.
PHOTO: GARLAND MARSHALL

Plate 4-4. Basting the quilt. PHOTO: GARLAND MARSHALL

Plate 4-5. Quilt with basting stitches showing.
PHOTO: GARLAND MARSHALL

plays, dance with the needle, going any direction you feel like at the time. (Plate 4-4)

It's important to get up and stretch every now and then because you'll probably get stiff while doing this. I hope you pick a day when you can have the carpet to yourself. Maybe even two days. Or at least train the family to walk around the quilt for a couple of days so that you don't have to do the basting all at once. I usually spend a full day or a day and a half when basting a large quilt, but I also do laundry, buy groceries, cook dinner, read the mail, pick flowers, and basically live in between the basting sessions.

When the basting is finished, it should look something like Plate 4-5.

Lifting the quilt from the carpet is fun. Little pop, pop, pop noises can be heard as the hairs from the carpet let go of the quilt. I have yet to actually baste the quilt to the carpet.

Turn the quilt over and be sure that it looks firmly basted on the back, too. Check to be satisfied that there aren't any wrinkles basted in. If it was stretched tightly and pinned securely to the carpet, this won't happen.

Now it's time to start quilting. Here's the neat part. Sit in your favorite chair, find the best light, go to a neighbor's house, prop up in bed, or take an airplane trip (if the quilt is small). The quilt is being held together by the basting stitches better than a lot of quilts are quilted! All you are doing is filling in with quilting stitches. (Plate 4-6, page 80)

If your quilt looks like it might get some wrinkles or creases quilted in, stop right away. Put the quilt down on a table or the floor, smooth out the fullness evenly in that part of the quilt, and add more basting stitches. Start quilting again and it will be okay.

Start your quilting stitches somewhere in the middle. The quilt is held together well enough with the basting that it doesn't really matter what part of the middle. I usually finish quilting the center of a quilt before I start the borders because, after I've filled the whole center with quilting, the basting stitches on the border look loose, and I sometimes have to tighten them up a bit. No problem —just place the borders on a flat surface, tighten up the basting stitches, or add more basting and continue quilting.

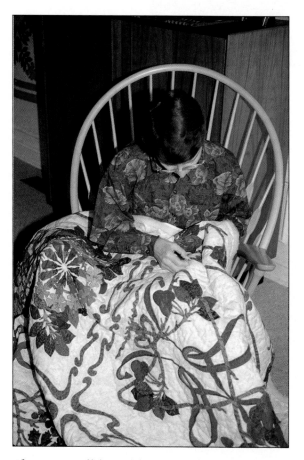

Plate 4-6. Quilting without a frame. PHOTO: GARLAND MARSHALL

THOUGHTS FROM GARLAND:

I suspect that this technique helps explain the small, regular stitches that characterize Suzanne's quilts, resulting in best workmanship awards, including the Gingher Prize at the AQS show. She can basically hold the needle still and manipulate the fabric with the other hand. It's quite different from using a frame. In fact, when her guild demonstrated quilting on a frame at a festival, she was hard-pressed to participate and produce quilting that met the guild's standards.

Designing
a Quilt
Block

SUZANNE MARSHALL

A pieced and appliquéd quilt made in New England in 1870, which was a traditional basket pattern filled with flowers and birds, inspired me to try to design my own traditional basket quilt. But I didn't want the quilt to look totally traditional. I wanted to jazz it up with unexpected surprises.

My quilt, *Bountiful Baskets*, has won several awards and received the comments shown below.

Designing *Bountiful Baskets* was so much fun, I'm sure that you can do it, too. It is not necessary to think of yourself as an artist. If you've cut flowers in a garden and arranged them in a vase, you can think about designing a quilt block with personal appliquéd touches the same way.

First, collect images of things that you like. Identification guides for flowers, trees, amphibians, fish, birds, mammals, and insects are wonderful resources. The library is a great place to start. Take a trip to the zoo with a camera and use images from your own photographs. Draw around real leaves. Look at postcards, wallpaper samples, old embroideries, and architectural details. Adapt and simplify the shapes you have drawn around and collected so that they can be used for appliqué. (Plate 5-1)

Save your collected paper patterns and keep them in a box or in plastic sheet protectors in a notebook. I like the sheet protectors because I can see through them and can organize my collected motifs so they are easier to find.

Decide on the size of your block and draw it on graph paper full-size. The blocks in *Bountiful Baskets* are 12" squares.

Negative Comments
    consider quilting in sashing and around baskets
    consider scale of borders

Positive Comments
    lays flat and straight
    great choice of fabrics—a lot of thought put into each block
    good combination of the original with the traditional
    interesting color combination
    variety in each square provides much interest
    delightful, I love it
    wonderful quilt; workmanship superb, colors well chosen, quilting very well done; very clever idea to enhance baskets with appliqué
    wonderful folk-art feel
    it's so refreshing to see such an interesting original design, especially combined with such a traditionally pieced block; the animals and insect appliqués are cleverly conceived and executed; the embroidery works well to highlight some of the little creatures; this is a fun piece to look at and, I'm sure, enjoy

Plate 5-1. Selected animals, leaves, and flower shapes, including Cass Gilbert's squirrel. Photo: Garland Marshall

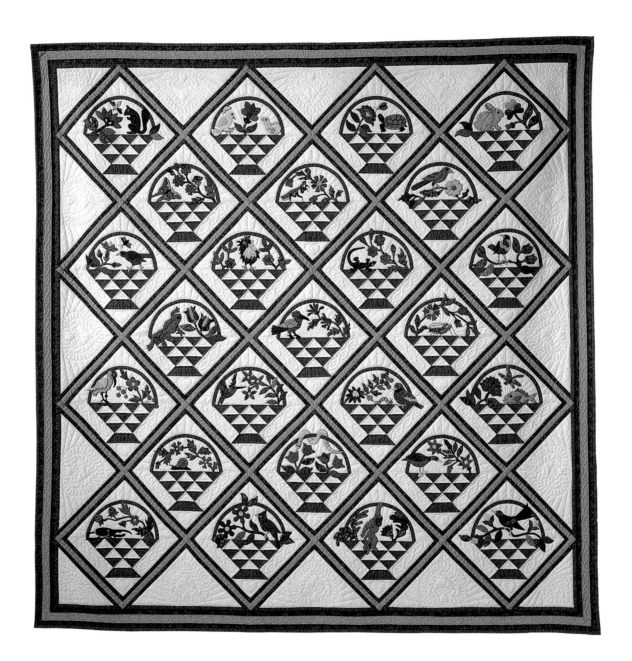

Plate 5-2. BOUNTIFUL BASKETS, 81" x 81", 1993.

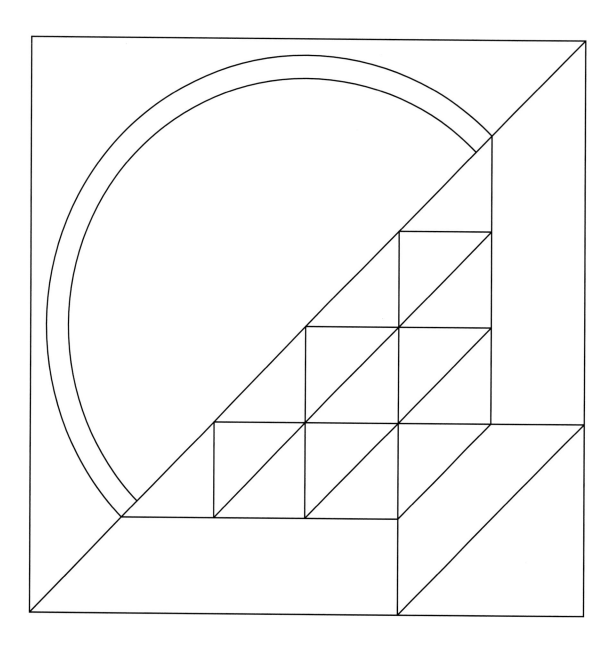

**Fig. 5-5. Pattern for the basket in the BOUNTIFUL
BASKETS blocks.**

TAKE-AWAY APPLIQUÉ

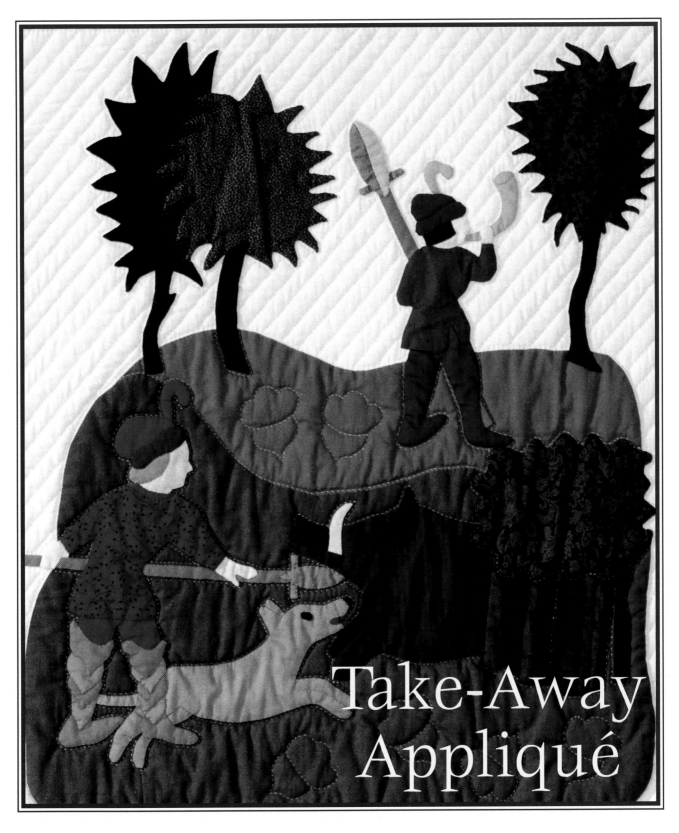

Take-Away
Appliqué

y first appliqué project was a mess! The edges weren't smooth, the points weren't pointy, and the inside curves had frays that tried to pop out and become part of the design on the front. Often, I'd try appliquéing a long leaf or stem and find that one side would sew down nicely, and while I was sewing the next side of the appliquéd piece, it would suddenly warp and get ripples. Why?

Another problem was trying to figure out how to appliqué a multi-pieced pattern. If I drew the entire piece on the background, I still couldn't figure out exactly where to sew each part because the fabric covered up some of the markings. Often I would have several pieces sewn down and then find that the next piece didn't cover up an edge that was supposed to be hidden. I'd have raw edges visible where they weren't supposed to show. I thought there must be a way. Would it be possible to do the appliqué without marking the background fabric at all?

Finally, I came up with a solution that works for me, and I've named it "Take-Away Appliqué" because it uses a "take-away" or "subtraction" method. It also uses a common household item, especially prevalent if there are school-age children in the family, *notebook paper*.

I love using notebook paper for templates because it is inexpensive and it has lines on it. I use the lines to match the grain lines on the appliqué piece with the grain lines on the background fabric. Not only do I like the look of matched grain lines, it solves warping and rippling problems on a long piece to be appliquéd. Of course, there are times when I want to use a particular directional fabric design for an appliqué piece. In this case, I simply disregard the grain lines

and let the fabric dictate the direction.

In order to stabilize the flimsy notebook paper templates while drawing around the edge onto the appliqué fabrics, use a piece of ¼" foam board. Pin the paper template through the fabric and into the foam board. The paper template will be held securely in place, making it easy to draw around the edges onto the fabric.

Try the small *Venetian Bird Wallhanging* to experiment with the Take-Away Appliqué method. The bird on this wallhanging was adapted from a mosaic floor in St. Mark's Cathedral, Venice, Italy.

Plate 6-1. Mosaic floor from St. Mark's Cathedral, Venice, Italy. PHOTO: SUZANNE MARSHALL

Plate 6-2. VENETIAN BIRD WALLHANGING, 27" x 27", 1996.

THOUGHTS FROM GARLAND:

As far as we can tell, this is a novel technique. No one in Suzanne's classes has been previously exposed to it. Baltimore Album appliqué expert Elly Sienkiewicz had not seen anyone else approach appliqué exactly in this fashion. So far, most, if not all, of Suzanne's students have responded enthusiastically, even those who only did patchwork. I believe it illustrates the principle that there is often a better way, but no one can teach it to you; otherwise, it would be the standard way.

Suzanne resisted teaching for several years. She simply resented the time away from doing her own creative projects. She wants the freedom to invest as much time in a project as she thinks it deserves or that she can tolerate.

VENETIAN BIRD WALLHANGING

SUPPLIES

- ⅝ yd. of background fabric
- 1 yd. of green for bias circle on wreath and border
- 32" strips of contrasting color for borders
- ⅛ yd. pieces of fabric or scraps of fabric that will work for the bird feathers and body
- ⅛ yd. of black for bird feet and beak
- ⅛ yd. for flowers
- thread to match fabric to be appliquéd
- several sheets of lined notebook paper
- small piece of foam board, at least as large as the bird pattern. A 10" x 10" piece will work just fine. I use ¼"-thick foam board, which can be found at office or art supply stores
- scissors to cut fabric and paper
- a soft, white Berol Prismacolor® pencil and a regular pencil. (The hard white Berol pencil that is usually sold at quilt shops doesn't work nearly as well for marking fabric as the soft Berol pencil that can be found at art supply stores.)

DIRECTIONS

- Cut a 19½" square of background fabric.
- Fold the square in half vertically, horizontally, and diagonally, either ironing or finger pressing the folds to make visible creases on the fabric. Now, it will be easy to find the center, and the crease lines on the fabric will make good guidelines for flower placement.
- Draw a circle 11" in diameter in the center of the square. (Plate 6-3)
- Trace the bird on lined notebook paper, being sure that the lines on the notebook paper go either horizontally or vertically across the bird. (Fig. 6-1, page 94)
- Cut out the notebook-paper pattern with paper-cutting scissors. (Plate 6-4)
- Place the paper pattern in the center of the circle exactly where you want the appliqué, making sure the lines on the notebook paper line up with the grain lines on the background fabric. Place a small, slightly visible mark on the background at the top of the bird's head and at the area on the body between the feet. This is all of the background marking you will have to do. (Plate 6-5)
- Cut out pattern piece 1, leaving the rest of the bird whole. (Plate 6-6)
- Select fabric for Feather 1. Place the fabric right side up on top of the foam board and pin the notebook-paper pattern piece through the fabric and into the foam board in several places, making sure that the lines on the notebook paper are lined up with the grain line on the fabric either vertically or horizontally.

Take-Away Appliqué

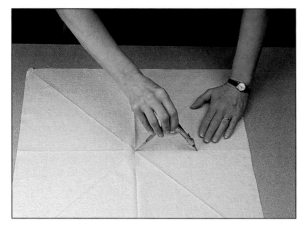

Plate 6-3. Draw a circle 11" in diameter on the background.

Plate 6-4. Cut out the notebook paper bird in one piece.

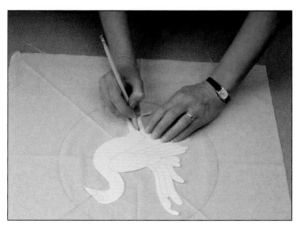

Plate 6-5. Make tiny marks on the background at the top of the head and between the feet.

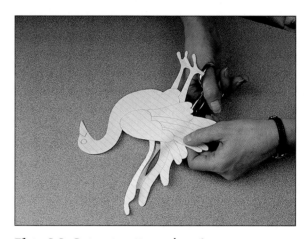

Plate 6-6. Cut out pattern piece 1.

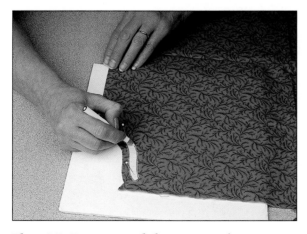

Plate 6-7. Draw around the pattern piece.

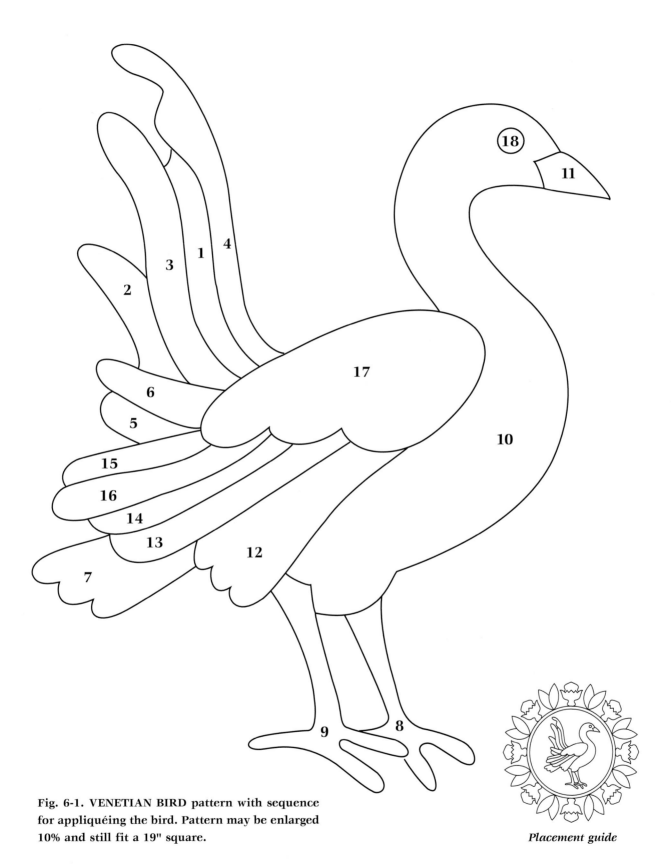

Fig. 6-1. VENETIAN BIRD pattern with sequence for appliquéing the bird. Pattern may be enlarged 10% and still fit a 19" square.

Placement guide

Take-Away Appliqué

Fig. 6-2. VENETIAN BIRD. One-fourth of wreath pattern surrounding the Venetian bird for a 19" square. Pattern may be enlarged 10% and still fit a 19" square.

- Draw around Feather 1 with a pencil. (Plate 6-7)
- Cut out the fabric feather, adding an approximate 3/16" turn-under allowance by eye when cutting. The parts of the feather that will be covered by other appliqué pieces should have at least a 1/4" allowance, which will not be turned under. The extra fabric will allow for slight errors in placement.
- Place the notebook-paper bird back on the background, checking the two marks to be sure the bird is placed in the same spot as before.
- Slip the fabric bird feather under the paper pattern in the gap left by the cut-out piece. (Plate 6-8) The grain lines on the fabric will help with proper placement, as they will line up with the lines on the notebook paper.
- Baste the appliqué in place with large stitches.
- Needle-turn the allowance.
- Follow the same procedure with Feather 2 and so on. As the pieces are cut from the notebook-paper bird pattern, the fabric appliqué pieces line up perfectly with the part that has been "taken away." (Plate 6-9)
- Several pieces can be basted on before being appliquéd as long as they are not on top of something that hasn't yet been sewn down. For instance, appliqué pieces for patterns 1, 2, 5, 7, and 8 could be basted down and then all needle-turned before adding 3, 4, and 9. (Plate 6-10)
- When all of the pieces of the bird have been appliquéd, the entire notebook-paper pattern piece will have been cut apart, but not until then. (Plates 6-11, 6-12, and 6-13)
- Optional: Using two strands of black embroidery thread, make an outline stitch through the background fabric right next to the edge of the appliquéd bird. Outline the entire bird and each of the feathers. (Fig. 6-3)
- You will need a piece of bias fabric nearly 1 yd. long for the circle in the wreath. I don't use bias bars or glue sticks, just an iron to prepare my bias for sewing.
- First, cut your fabric in half on the bias.

Plate 6-8. The fabric bird feather goes in the gap left in the paper pattern piece.

Plate 6-9. Two feathers have been appliquéd.

Plate 6-10. Pattern pieces 1, 2, 5, 7, and 8 are in place.

Plate 6-11. As the pieces from the paper pattern are "taken-away," the fabric appliqué pieces line up perfectly with what is left.

Plate 6-12. Continue cutting the piece from the paper pattern.

Plate 6-13. Substitute fabric pieces for paper patterns.

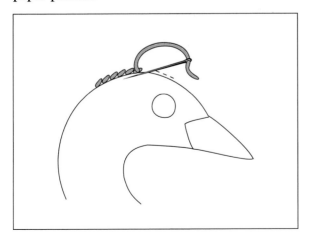

Fig. 6-3. Outline embroidery on VENETIAN BIRD.

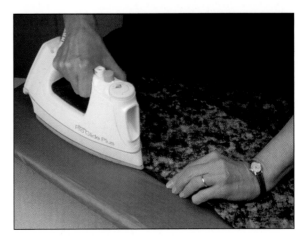

Plate 6-14. Press a ¼" turn-under seam on one bias edge of the cloth.

- Press a ¼" turn-under allowance on one bias edge of the cloth. (Plate 6-14)
- Make another fold the width of the bias strip that you want (I used a ½" width for the circle on the wreath) and press again. (Plate 6-15)
- Baste between the folds, catching all three layers with your basting stitches. (Plate 6-16)
- Turn the folded fabric back and cut it close to the basting stitches on the underside of the bias strip. (Plate 6-17)
- Now you have a piece of perfectly basted bias that can be manipulated any way you want.
- Place the bias strip on the circle and sew. (Plate 6-18)
- Cut out both parts of the flower from notebook paper. Follow the same procedure for the flower as for the bird, using the bottom half of the notebook paper as a guide for placing the top half of the flower, which needs to be appliquéd first. The horizontal, vertical, and diagonal creases on the background will indicate where the flowers should be placed. (Fig. 6-2, page 95)
- Place the paper pattern next to the bias circle and slip the blossom under it for perfect alignment. (Plate 6-19)
- Select leaves to be placed between the flowers. (Plate 6-20)
- Appliqué leaves between the flowers.
- Sew a 1" border around the piece.
- The piece measures 21" x 21". You can select any patchwork pattern that uses multiples of 3" for a fancy border. Finish with more borders, if desired. (Plate 6-21 and Fig. 6-4, page 100)

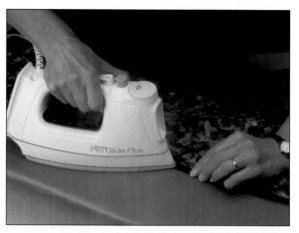

Plate 6-15. Fold the width of the bias strip that you want (I used a ½" width for the circle on the wreath) and press again.

Plate 6-16. Baste, catching both turn-under edges with your basting stitches.

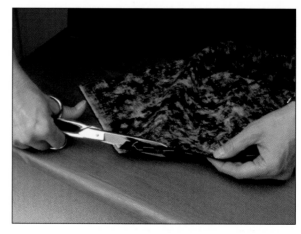

Plate 6-17. Turn the folded fabric back and cut close to the basting stitches on the underside of the bias strip.

Plate 6-18. Place the bias strip on the circle and sew.

Plate 6-19. Place the paper pattern next to the bias circle and slip the blossom under it for perfect alignment.

Plate 6-20. Select leaves to be placed between the flowers.

Plate 6-21. Color and border variation for VENETIAN BIRD.

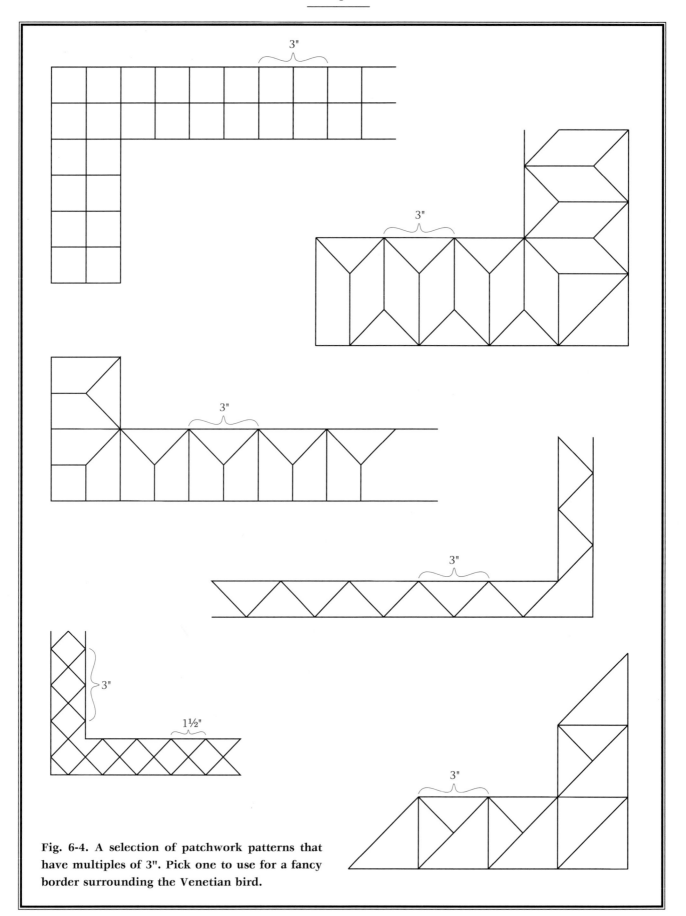

Fig. 6-4. A selection of patchwork patterns that have multiples of 3". Pick one to use for a fancy border surrounding the Venetian bird.

Plate 6-22. LOVE BIRDS WALLHANGING, 29" x
29", 1996. The quilt, MARSHALL MENAGERIE,
has several blocks that can be used as the center
of a wallhanging. One of the blocks that was
adapted from a mosaic floor tile in St. Mark's
Cathedral in Venice seemed especially appropriate for making a special quilted wedding gift. The
couple who received it named it LOVE BIRDS.

LOVE BIRDS WALLHANGING

SUPPLIES

- 1 yd. of background fabric
- ¼ yd. green fabric for leaves
- ⅛ yd. pieces of fabric or scraps of fabric for bird, basket, flowers, and patchwork borders
- 32" strips of contrasting fabric for borders
- thread to match fabric to be appliquéd
- several sheets of lined notebook paper
- small piece of foam board at least as large as the bird pattern
- paper and fabric scissors
- a soft, white Berol Prismacolor® pencil and a regular pencil

DIRECTIONS

- Trace the pattern from the following pages or photocopy the pages and tape them together to form the complete pattern. Reverse the bird and flower patterns on either side of the basket and main stem.
- Trace the pattern on the background fabric, using a marker that can be removed when washed. Not all of the details of the pattern need to be marked. The beak on the bird and the end of one tail feather, the tip of the flowers, and the bottom of the basket are the only things that need to be marked.
- *For directions on the Take-Away method of appliqué, refer to the illustrations accompanying the* Venetian Bird Wallhanging *pages 93, 96–99.*
- Trace one bird from the pattern, Fig. 6-5, page 103, on lined notebook paper, being sure that the lines on the notebook paper go either horizontally or vertically across the bird.
- Cut out the notebook-paper bird pattern with paper-cutting scissors.
- Cut out pattern piece 1 (a foot), leaving the rest of the paper bird whole.
- Select fabric for foot 1, place the fabric right side up on top of the foam board and pin the notebook-paper pattern piece through the fabric and into the foam board in several places, making sure that the lines on the notebook paper are lined up with the grain line on the fabric either vertically or horizontally.
- Draw around the pattern piece with a pencil.

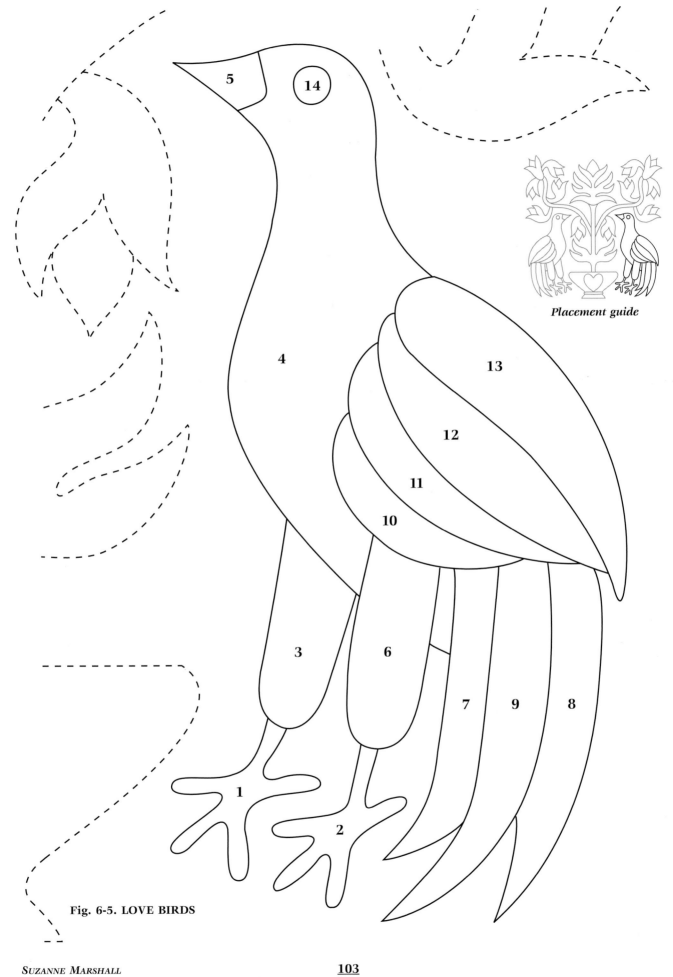

Fig. 6-5. LOVE BIRDS

Placement guide

- Cut out the appliqué piece, adding approximately $\frac{3}{16}$" turn-under allowance when cutting. Leave at least $\frac{1}{4}$" allowance at the top of the bird foot. The extra fabric will allow for slight errors in placement.
- Place the notebook-paper bird on the background in its proper position, lining up the pattern with the beak and tail feather marks on the background, and making sure that the lines on the paper are once again lined up with the grain lines on the background.
- Place the fabric bird foot on the background, slipping it under the paper pattern at the spot where the paper was cut away. The grain lines on the fabric will help with proper placement, because they should match the grain lines on the background. The $\frac{1}{4}$" fabric allowance at the top of the fabric bird foot will slip underneath the paper pattern to position it properly.
- Baste the appliqué in place with large stitches.
- Needle-turn the allowance.

- Follow the same procedure with Foot 2, then Leg 3, and then the body. As the pieces are cut from the notebook-paper bird pattern, the fabric appliqué pieces line up perfectly with the part that has been taken away. Always place what is left of the paper pattern piece back on the fabric to be sure that everything is lined up.
- When all of the pieces of the bird have been appliquéd, the entire notebook-paper pattern will have been cut apart, but not until then. Following the same instructions, appliqué the reversed second bird in place.
- The flower sections may be appliquéd in the same fashion as the birds. The basket with the heart will be the last piece to be sewn. (Figs. 6-7, 6-8, and 6-9, pages 105–107)
- Sew a 1" border around the piece.
- The piece should measure 21" x 21". Select any patchwork pattern that uses multiples of 3" and use it to add a fancy border. (Figs. 6-4 and 6-6) Finish with another 1" border around the outside.

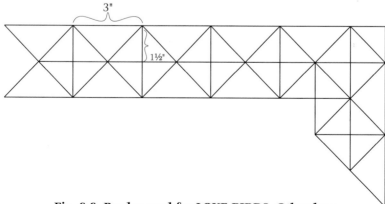

Fig. 6-6. Border used for LOVE BIRDS. Other borders using multiples of 3" may be found in Fig. 6-4, page 100.

Placement guide

Fig. 6-7. LOVE BIRDS, pages 105–107.

Fig. 6-8 and 6-9 (opposite page). LOVE BIRDS
continued.

Placement guide

TAKE-AWAY APPLIQUÉ

Placement guide

Tacuinum Sanitatis, Natural History magazine. courtesy of the
Spencer Collection, The New York Public Library, Astor, Lenox
and Tilden Foundation.

Appliquéd
Patchwork

By now it must be obvious that I love incorporating animals, birds, bugs, fish, and wildlife into my quilt designs. I started *Earth Watch* with a few of my collected paper animal pattern pieces. I drew a few small squares and used animals as the basis for each design.

Thinking about my earlier Japanese quilts, which were designed to showcase the special yukata fabrics in a traditional patchwork block, I decided to use the same idea to give small appliquéd blocks some added pizzazz. I selected Flower Pot (*Grandmother Clark's Authentic Early American Quilts*, 1932) because of the large block in the middle of the patchwork square.

Another challenge to myself was to have part of the appliqué go beyond the borders and into the patchwork to make the block appear more dimensional. It also helps tie the appliqué and patchwork together to make a more cohesive block.

When I was about halfway through sewing the appliquéd patchwork blocks, we took a trip to South Africa and Madagascar. We photographed wildlife (Plates 7-1 through 7-4) while we were traveling, and I adapted some of them to use in the quilt. (Plate 7-5, page 111)

Plate 7-1. Sifaka lemur in Madagascar, lemur on quilt, fifth row, far right. PHOTO: SUZANNE MARSHALL

Plate 7-2. Antelope in Kruger Park, South Africa, antelope on quilt, second row, far right. PHOTO: SUZANNE MARSHALL

Plate 7-3. Rhinoceroses in Mkhaya Reserve, Swaziland, rhinoceroses on quilt, fourth row, far left. PHOTO: SUZANNE MARSHALL

Plate 7-4. Ring-tailed lemur in Berenty Reserve, Madagascar, lemur on quilt, center of bottom border. PHOTO: GARLAND MARSHALL

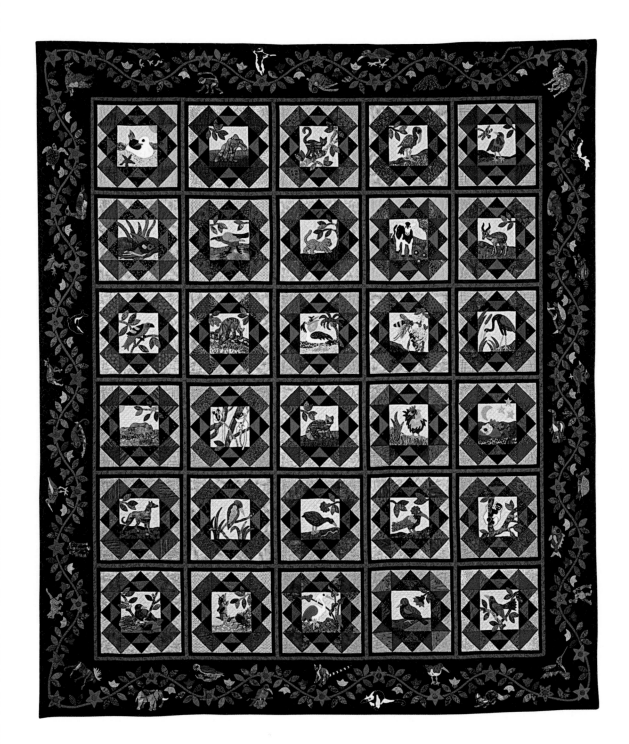

Plate 7-5. EARTH WATCH, 83" x 96", 1997.

Plate 7-6. APPLIQUÉD PATCHWORK WALLHANGING, 34" x 34", 1997.

APPLIQUÉD PATCHWORK WALLHANGING

Try sewing a small wallhanging using four of the *Earth Watch* blocks. The completed wallhanging will be 34" x 34". Choose any 12" patchwork block that has a 6" block in the center to be used for the appliqué. (Fig 7-1)

FABRIC

- ¼ yd. of background fabric for the appliqué; this will be the center of the patchwork star.
- ⅛ yd. pieces of fabric or scraps of fabric that will work for the animals or birds selected for the appliqué
- scraps of various green fabrics for leaves and grass
- ¼ yd. of four different fabrics for the patchwork stars
- 1 yd. black fabric for border, lattice strips, and binding. This may also be used for one of the patchwork star fabrics.

SUPPLIES

- thread to match fabric to be appliquéd
- several sheets of lined notebook paper
- fabric and paper-cutting scissors
- a soft, white Berol Prismacolor® pencil and a regular pencil: the hard white Berol pencil that is usually sold at quilt shops doesn't work nearly as well for marking fabric as the soft Berol pencil that can be found at art supply stores
- black embroidery thread
- small piece of foam board at least as large as the appliqué animal or bird
- sewing supplies

DIRECTIONS

The directions given are for the Dawdling Duck block, shown in Plate 7-6, page 112, row 1, block 1. The directions can be adjusted to apply to the other appliquéd patchwork as well.

For directions on the Take-Away method of appliqué, refer to the illustrations accompanying the Venetian Bird Wallhanging *in Chapter 6, pages 93, 96–99.*

- Cut a 6½" square of background fabric to be used behind the appliqué.
- Trace the grass from the pattern on lined notebook paper, making sure that the lines on the notebook paper go either horizontally or vertically across the design.
- Cut out the notebook-paper pattern with paper-cutting scissors.
- Place grass fabric right side up on top of the foam board. Pin the notebook-paper pattern piece through the fabric and into the foam board, making sure that the lines on the notebook paper

are lined up with the grain line on the fabric.

- Draw around the pattern piece with a pencil.
- Cut out the appliqué piece, adding ³⁄₁₆" of fabric by eye around the edges for a turn-under allowance. Leave at least ¼" allowance in those areas that will be covered by the other appliqué.
- Appliqué the grass in place.
- Appliqué the small stem in the upper

right corner of the block.

- Select a 12" patchwork block to use for appliquéd patchwork. (Fig. 7-1) The patchwork can be completed now. Use the 6" block with the grass and stem in place as the center of the design.
- Using more notebook paper, trace around the duck and cut out with paper-cutting scissors.
- Select fabric for the duck foot nearest the worm (because part of it is behind

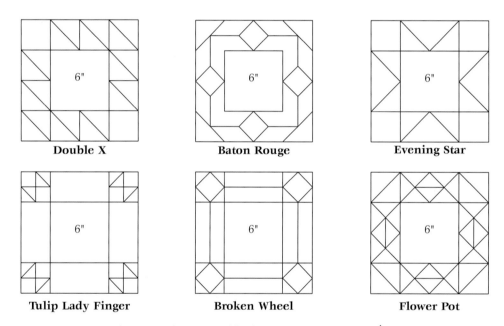

Double X Baton Rouge Evening Star

Tulip Lady Finger Broken Wheel Flower Pot

Fig. 7-1. Select a 12" block to use for APPLIQUÉD PATCHWORK.

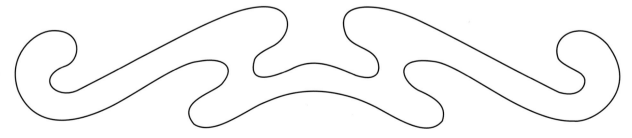

Fig. 7-2. Border used for the CRAFTY CRANE miniature (enlarge to fit desired border).

the other foot), and draw around the paper template. Cut out the appliqué fabric piece, adding approximate ³⁄₁₆" turn-under allowance when cutting.

- Place the notebook-paper duck on the background, positioning it in the desired place on the grass.

- Slip the fabric duck foot under the paper pattern in the gap left by the cut-out piece. The grain lines on the fabric will help with proper placement, as they will line up with the lines on the notebook paper.

- Appliqué the duck foot.

- Proceed with the second duck foot. Continue piece by piece, until the duck has been completed. When all of the pieces of the duck have been appliquéd, the entire notebook paper pattern piece will be cut apart, but not until then.

- The worm and flower may be appliquéd now.

- Appliqué the leaves on the stem, going beyond the borders of the 6" block into the patchwork.

- Make an embroidered French knot for the worm's eye and a small stitch for his tongue. (I seriously doubt that worms have tongues.)

- After completing all four blocks, sew ½" borders around each finished block. Strips of fabric should be 1" wide before sewn.

- Use red lattice strips to connect the blocks. The strips of fabric should be 1" wide before sewn.

- Cut 3" borders out of the black fabric to complete the wallhanging.

- The quilting pattern for the flower pot

block in *Earth Watch* is on page 116. (Fig. 7-4)

EARTH WATCH MINIATURES

Make a miniature quilt by enlarging one of the *Earth Watch* patterns. Add borders to make the desired size. The Crafty Crane border (Fig. 7-2, page 114) may be enlarged to fit.

Plate 7-7. CRAFTY CRANE, 16" x 16", 1997.

Fig. 7-3 (above). Crafty Crane block from EARTH WATCH, shown at 50%. Photocopy at 200%.

Fig. 7-4 (left). Quilting pattern used for the flower pot block in EARTH WATCH.

DESIGN YOUR OWN APPLIQUÉD PATCHWORK BLOCK

• Draw a 6" x 6" square on a piece of paper.

• Place the animal or bird (Figs. 7-5 through 7-8) that you want to use in the 6" x 6" square and draw grass, water, or tree branches that would be appropriate for the animal. Grass doesn't have to be much more than a sloping line.

• Draw the animal in place.

• Fill in with leaves, remembering to draw some of them outside the lines of the square so that they will go beyond the border into the patchwork.

Fig. 7-5.

Fig. 7-6.

TAKE-AWAY APPLIQUÉ – SUZANNE MARSHALL

Fig. 7-7.

Fig. 7-8.

TAKE-AWAY APPLIQUÉ – SUZANNE MARSHALL

Patterns
and
Images

Designing a quilt is a lot of fun, and searching for patterns and motifs to use in interesting ways adds to the delight of quiltmaking.

Some of my favorite patterns have been used in several quilts. Cass Gilbert's squirrel can be found in *Cass Gilbert Remembered*, *Friends*, *Full Bloom*, and *Bountiful Baskets*. The squirrel is the same, but it was enlarged or reduced with a photocopy machine so that it would fit the spot where I wanted to use it.

The bugs in *Bed Bugs* and *Don't Bug Me!* can be used in either quilt. The dragonflies appear on *Dragonflowers* as well as *Full Bloom* and *Marshall Menagerie*. *Adam and Eve* and *Marshall Menagerie* have the same sea-horse appliquéd on them. Several of the birds in *Bountiful Baskets* can also be found on *Earth Watch*.

It is, therefore, quite possible to use the same images in different quilts. Variations in size, color, fabrics, and surroundings make the patterns look different from one quilt to another. It is also possible to change the leaves on a flower, the wings on a bird, or the direction an animal is facing. Try to embellish the patterns and make them your own.

The following chapter contains a selection of patterns from many of my quilts. Feel free to choose a motif that appeals to you and use a variation of it in something that you are making.

Fig. 8-1.

Fig. 8-2.

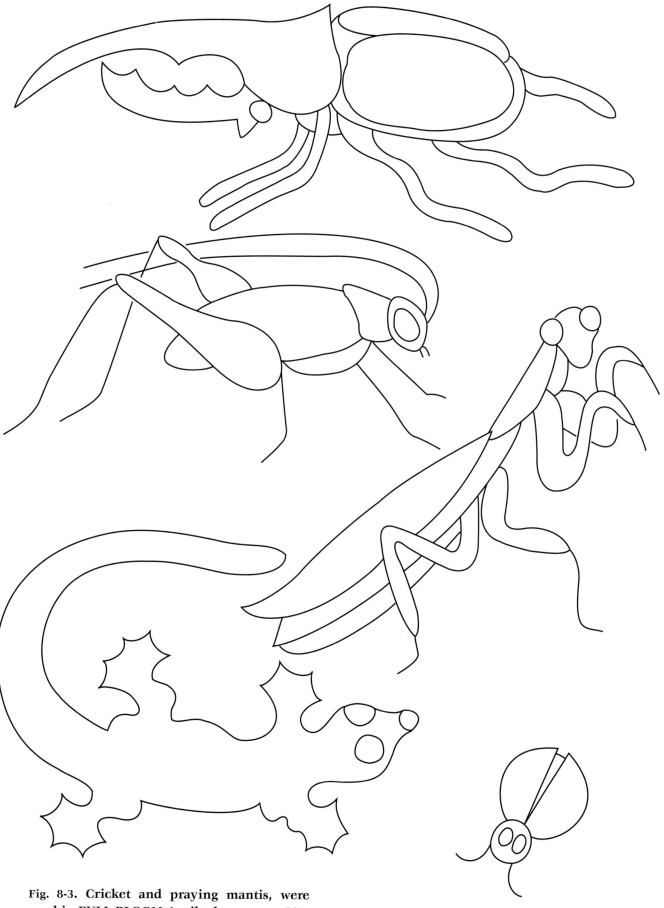

Fig. 8-3. Cricket and praying mantis, were
used in FULL BLOOM (quilt shown page 38).

Fig. 8-4.

Fig. 8-5.

Fig. 8-6. Squirrel and grape leaves from CASS GILBERT REMEMBERED, quilt shown page 34.

Fig. 8-7. Bird from CASS GILBERT REMEM-
BERED, quilt shown page 34.

TAKE-AWAY APPLIQUÉ – SUZANNE MARSHALL

Fig. 8-8. Keith, with roller skates, climbing a
tree from FRIENDS (quilt shown page 37).

Fig. 8-9. Raccoon and duck, from FRIENDS
(quilt shown page 37).

Take-Away Appliqué – Suzanne Marshall

**Fig. 8-10. Chris feeding the ducks, from
FRIENDS (quilt shown page 37).**

Fig. 8-11. Lee with his pet snake, from FRIENDS (quilt shown page 37).

Take-Away Appliqué – Suzanne Marshall

Fig. 8-12. Melissa with insects, from FRIENDS (quilt shown page 37).

Fig. 8-13. Mother bird with nest, from
FRIENDS (quilt shown page 37).

Fig. 8-14. Sea gull, from SILVER GULL BEACH
(quilt shown page 40).

Fig. 8-15. Sea gull, from SILVER GULL BEACH (quilt shown page 40).

Fig. 8-16. Sea gull and shells, from SILVER
GULL BEACH (quilt shown page 40).

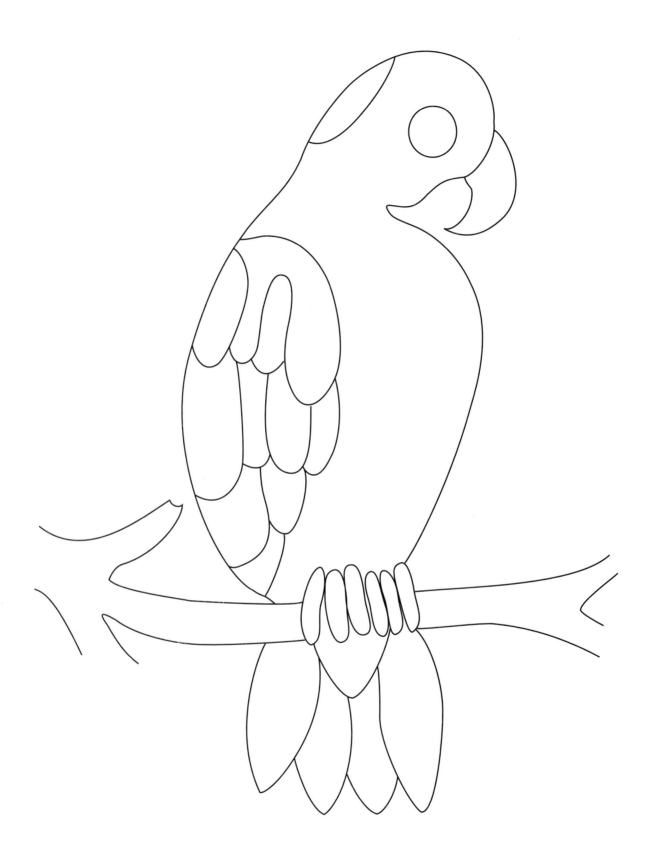

Fig. 8-17. Parrot, from JOURNEY THROUGH
TIME (quilt shown page 49).

TAKE-AWAY APPLIQUÉ – SUZANNE MARSHALL

Fig. 8-18. Deer, from JOURNEY THROUGH
TIME (quilt shown page 49).

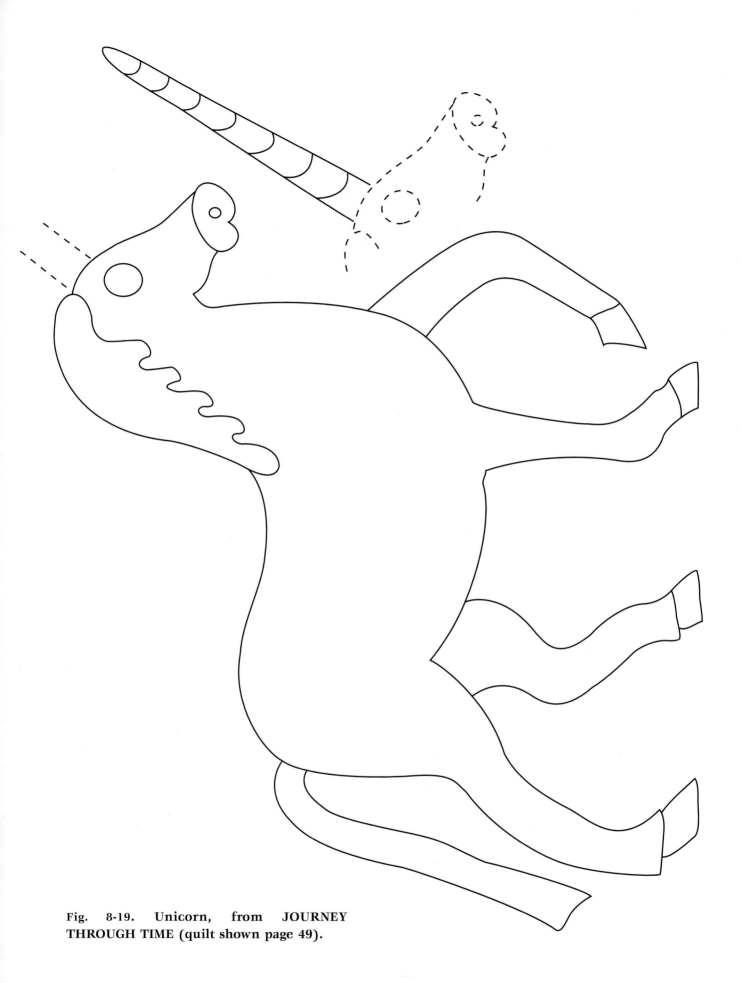

Fig. 8-19. Unicorn, from JOURNEY
THROUGH TIME (quilt shown page 49).

Fig. 8-20. Flower and ladybug, from JOURNEY THROUGH TIME (quilt shown page 49).

Fig. 8-21. Zinnia, from JOURNEY THROUGH
TIME (quilt shown page 49).

Fig. 8-22. Butterflies and caterpillar, from
JOURNEY THROUGH TIME (quilt shown
page 49).

Fig. 8-23. Flower and butterfly, from JOUR-
NEY THROUGH TIME (quilt shown page 49).

**Fig. 8-24. Goat, from JOURNEY THROUGH
TIME (quilt shown page 49).**

Fig. 8-25. Daffodil, from JOURNEY THROUGH
TIME (quilt shown page 49).

Take-Away Appliqué – Suzanne Marshall

Fig. 8-26. One-fourth of BED BUGS. Wreath for an 18" square. (BED BUGS quilt shown page 52).

Fig. 8-27. Bugs and flowers, from BED BUGS
(quilt shown page 52).

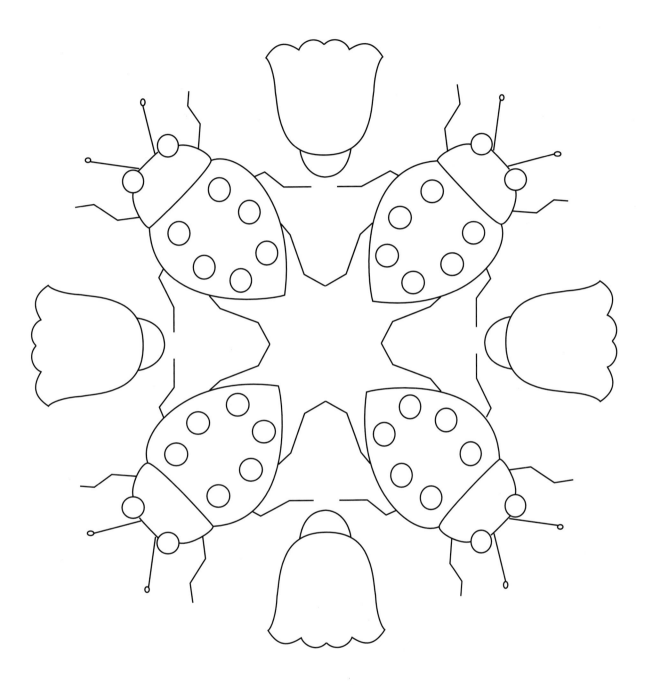

Fig. 8-28. Bugs and flowers, from BED BUGS
(quilt shown page 52).

Fig. 8-29. Bugs and flowers, from BED BUGS
(quilt shown page 52).

Fig. 8-30. Peacock with flower, from ADAM
AND EVE (quilt shown page 59).

Fig. 8-31. Birds, from ADAM AND EVE (quilt shown page 59).

TAKE-AWAY APPLIQUÉ – SUZANNE MARSHALL

Fig. 8-32. One-fourth of 18" block from DON'T BUG ME (quilt shown page 66).

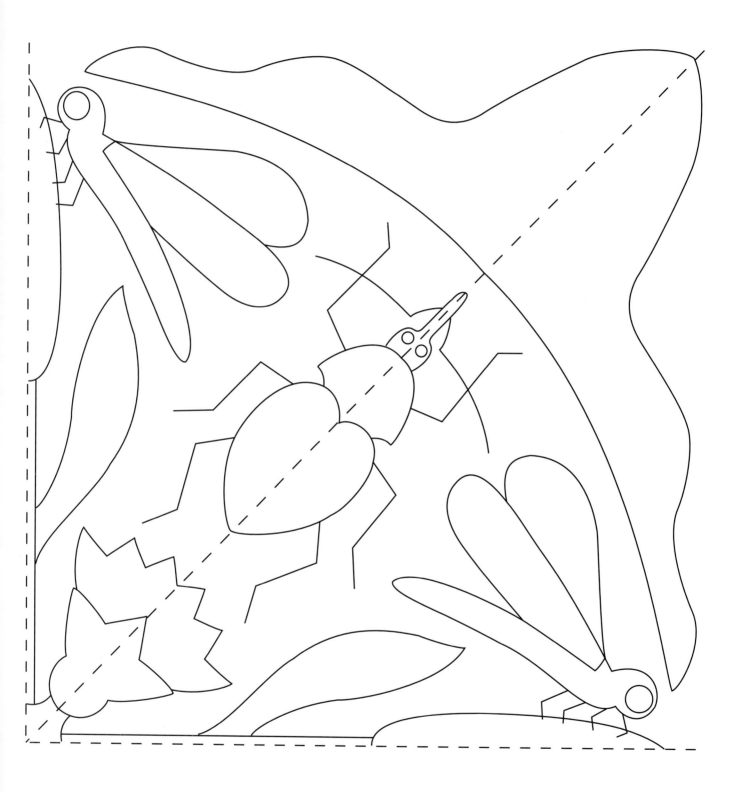

Fig. 8-33. One-fourth of 18" block from DON'T
BUG ME (quilt shown page 66).

Fig. 8-34. One-fourth of 18" block from DON'T
BUG ME (quilt shown page 66).

Fig. 8-35. One-fourth of 18" block from DON'T
BUG ME (quilt shown page 66).

TAKE-AWAY APPLIQUÉ – SUZANNE MARSHALL

Fig. 8-36. One-fourth of 18" block from DON'T BUG ME (quilt shown page 66).

Fig. 8-37. One-fourth of 18" block from DON'T
BUG ME (quilt shown page 66).

Fig. 8-38. Design your own 18" block. Mix and match the flowers and bugs.

Fig. 8-39. Design your own 18" block. Mix and match the flowers and bugs.

Fig. 8-40. Design your own 18" block. Mix and match the flowers and bugs.

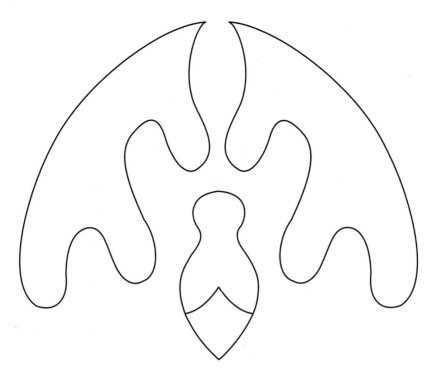

Fig. 8-41. Design your own 18" block. Mix and match the flowers and bugs.

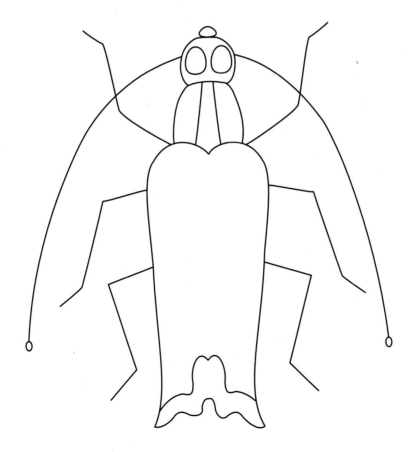

Dawdling duck

Buxom bird

Blundering bird

Coy crane

Fig. 8-42. The patterns on pages 163–168 are from EARTH WATCH (quilt shown on page 111). All of these blocks are shown at 50%. Please photocopy at 200%.

Wily warbler

Hopeful hoopoe bird

Cranky kingfisher

Sunning sea gull

Elegant egret

Pesky pelican

Nurturing nester

Cocky rooster

Glib grouper

Rhinoceros relatives

Anxious antelope

Munching moo cow

Furtive fox

Dubious dog

Fishing fosa

Leaping leopard

Busy bugs

Limber lemur

Leering lemur

Frollicking lemurs

Questions
and
Answers

Invariably, when I give quilt lectures, there are questions from the audience. These are the ones most frequently asked:

Why are you willing to share negative comments about your quilts?

I have learned so much from the judge's comments, and feel that maybe other people can learn from them, too. Many of the criticisms are valid and have helped me improve my quilts. Other criticisms seem ridiculous to me, and I ignore them. After all, I am making my quilts to satisfy myself, not to please the judges. For example, if I am happy with the colors in a quilt, it doesn't matter to me if a judge thinks the colors should be different. I am the person who will live with the quilt, not the judge.

Do you wear a thimble?

Yes, I wear a thimble on my right hand to push the needle through the three layers. I do not wear a thimble on my left hand, because I want to feel the needle come through the layers. If my finger gets sore under the quilt, I wrap it in a couple of layers of electrical tape to help protect it. The electrical tape helps keep my finger from getting sore, and I can still feel the needle.

Many of your appliqué motifs look stuffed. Are they?

No, I've found that, if I have lots of quilting in the background, it makes the appliqué appear to stand away from it, tending to make the appliqué look stuffed.

Do you cut out behind your appliqué?

Sometimes. If I plan to quilt inside the appliqué, I try to cut the background out from behind it so that I will have fewer layers for my quilting needle to go through. If I do not plan to quilt an appliqué piece, I usually leave the background behind it.

How much fabric do you buy?

I usually buy half-yard pieces unless I'm buying a background or backing. Nearly always, I have the squares for a quilt finished before I know how I plan to join them or what kind of border to use. I then take the squares or pieces into a shop to pick out the amount of fabric I'll need to use for lattice strips or borders.

How do you appliqué inside curves?

First, clip to the marked seam allowance line at inside angles and corners. Stop stitching at least ¼" before the inside curve. Turn the seam allowance under ¼" after the inside curve and hold it down with your thumb. Sweep the edge of the needle between your thumb and the last appliqué stitch, smoothly turning under the fabric. Hold the turned-under fabric down with your thumb and stitch.

How do you make sharp points:

I follow five steps to make sharp points:
- Stitch to the exact place where you want the point to be.
- Turn the top fabric back and trim the seam allowance that is underneath on a diagonal. Even trimming a couple of threads will help eliminate bulk.
- Turn the fabric under straight back at the point.
- Turn the fabric under beyond the point.
- Pull on the thread to extend the point and stitch. Pulling on the thread really helps pull a sharp point out.

Why are my appliqué stitches sometimes visible on the front of the quilt?

First, be sure you are using thread that matches the color of fabric you are appliquéing. Sometimes the appliqué stitches need to be tightened a bit. Try to pull on them with your needle on the wrong side of the background fabric to see if they are loose. Check the front to see if this helped to make the visible threads disappear. If it did, try to make your appliqué stitches a bit tighter.

It's possible that a slanted stitch was made on the front, like a whipping stitch. The needle needs to go into the background right next to the place where the thread comes out of the appliqué. If the needle is moved forward before going into the background instead of right next to where the thread comes out, a slanted stitch will be made that will more likely show on the front. The needle should move forward about ¹⁄₁₆" to ¹⁄₈" underneath the background fabric, coming up and catching only a thread or two on the edge of the folded seam allowance of the appliqué before going back into the background right next to that spot.

The eyes on the appliquéd animals are little circles? How do you appliqué such tiny circles?

First, I draw a small circle on the fabric to be appliquéd and cut it out with a ¹⁄₈" seam allowance. I tack it in place with a couple of tiny stitches in the center of the circle so that it will be stabilized while stitching. Bringing the needle up from the wrong side of the fabric and coming through right on the marked line, I turn the seam allowance under and take the first stitch. Then with the point of the needle I turn under just enough fabric to take one more stitch, holding it down with my thumbnail until the stitch is taken. I proceed around the circle in the same fashion, remembering that I only have to take one stitch at a time. Knowing that only enough of the seam allowance has to be turned under for one stitch makes all the difference.

What kind of batting do you use?

I usually use thin batts because I have better luck making small stitches. I have always used polyester because my needle slides through them better than cotton batts, and I want my quilting to be fun, not a struggle. However, there are some new cotton batts that I am tempted to try.

What kind of thread do you use?

I usually use cotton-covered polyester hand quilting thread for quilting. An all purpose thread, which is also a cotton-covered polyester, is just fine for me when I appliqué.

I dislike 100 percent polyester thread. I have occasionally used it for a small piece of appliqué when I haven't been able to match a fabric color with cotton. It's hard to thread a needle with it, and I feel that it might slice into my 100% cotton fabric.

How do you finish a thread when quilting?

I usually stitch through the batting to a seam line or next to an appliqué piece. Then I hide a couple of backstitches there. If it is in the middle of background quilting where there isn't a seam or appliqué piece to hide the backstitches, I have the needle travel to another stitch and I hide a backstitch under that stitch. I then make a knot to pull through to hide in the batting. Or the needle can travel to an area that will be quilted later, and I take a couple of nearly invisible backstitches right on the quilting line. The quilting that goes over this area will go right over the thread and make it impossible to pull out.

What needle do you use for quilting?

My favorite needle for quilting is an English needle made of solid stainless steel and is a size 10 between. There are 10 in a package and they are sold in little wooden needle cases. Even though the needle is very short, the eye is still large enough for me to thread.

What needle do you use for appliqué?

I use the same needle for appliqué that I use for quilting. I like the little, short needle because I can make better stitches. I have had students who have had trouble making stitches using long, appliqué needles. When they try the little short needles, most of them have told me it improves their stitches and makes the appliqué process easier.

What do you use to mark your quilting lines?

As you know from reading the judge's comments, I used to use an ordinary pencil. After reading the criticisms, I knew I needed to try something else. Besides, I once used a pencil that didn't wash out of the fabric, and that discouraged me from ever using a pencil again. In 1988, I started using a water soluble marking pen. I know this is controversial, but at this point, I have not had any trouble with marks coming back or the fabric deteriorating.

I do follow some guidelines: Always test the fabric with the pen first to see if the marks will come out. Try to mark very lightly so the mark does not go through to the batting. Do not leave the marks on for a long time and wipe them off with a wet cloth as the quilting is done. Do not expose the marks to heat from either sunshine or an iron. Do not use any detergents on a quilt that has marks from a water soluble pen. When the quilt is finished, put it in the washing machine in plain water

(no soaps) and agitate on the gentle cycle. I feel that the water moving back and forth through the quilt will take out any residual chemicals from the pen.

On dark fabrics, I like to use a soft white Berol Prismacolor® pencil. The markings show up plainly, and they rub off by the time the quilting is finished. Because it is a soft pencil, it must be sharpened rather frequently.

Do you do all of the marking on a quilt before it is layered with the batting?

No, I mark just one part at a time right before quilting in that section. I do this because I usually don't know what quilting I will use on the entire quilt. I tend to figure it out as I go.

An example of an exception to this, however, is the quilted feather pattern on *Cass Gilbert Remembered*. I traced that design on the muslin before layering the quilt.

How do you mark long straight lines like the ones making the diamonds in the background quilting for Full Bloom, Anniversary Quilt, *or* Journey Through Time?

I buy wooden moldings at the hardware store the width that I want to use. I have long wooden moldings in ½", ⅝", and ¾" widths. I place the molding diagonally across the quilt from corner to corner and mark next to the edge of the molding. I then move it across the quilt, lining it up with the previously marked line each time. Be sure to check the moldings to see that they are straight before buying them. (Plate 9-1)

How do you wash and dry your quilts?

When I first started making quilts, they were for our children and needed to be washed frequently. I threw them in the washing machine and dryer, and they came out beautifully. The only "disaster" I had at that time was a quilt that I had made mixing some brand new unwashed fabrics with some older fabrics that had been washed many times. The new fabrics shrank, causing stress within the quilt.

I still put the quilts in the washing machine on the gentle cycle, and I still use the dryer, but the quilts are tumbled in the machine using a low temperature and little heat. I take them out of the dryer before they are completely dry and lay them out flat across a bed or on the floor on a white sheet where they finish drying. Remember, I'm not talking about antique quilts.

How do you store your quilts?

We have a guest bedroom with a queen size bed in it. I layer the quilts one on top of the other on the bed. I put a bedspread on top of all of them so that the light doesn't damage any of the fabrics.

When we have guests, I have to fold the quilts and store them in a closet. I don't like to keep them folded for a long time, because I don't want crease lines to become visible. When the guests leave, back they go on top of the bed again.

Do you have any advice for new quilters?

Try to make a design your own even if it is a traditional pattern. You might incorporate something personal within a design or add your own creativity by changing a pattern some way. Perhaps you could use a piece of special fabric that may remind you of a person or an event to make a quilt more meaningful to you and your family.

Have fun! If working on a quilt causes stress, put it away for awhile. Taking it out later may give you a different perspective.

Plate 9-1. Marking JOURNEY THROUGH TIME, using a wooden molding strip. PHOTO: GARLAND MARSHALL

index of quilts

about
the author

Suzanne Marshall traces her development as a quilter to a library book and her collection of fabric scraps, gathered through many years of making clothes. Her first quilts were utilitarian, increasing in size with the growth of her children. Only in the mid-1980s did this self-taught quilter begin to design decorative quilts.

She entered her first local contest in 1985 and her first national competition in 1988. Recognition came rapidly after that. She has received many coveted awards, among them a first place in professional appliqué and the Gingher Award for Best Hand Workmanship at American Quilter's Society shows; grand prizes for three consecutive years from Better Homes and Gardens Books, awarded at International Quilt Festival in Houston, Texas; and first prize at Quilt Expo III in the Hague, Holland. Her quilt Soul of Medieval Italy was featured in an exhibit at the Museum of American Folk Art in New York City.

Suzanne was born in Joplin, Missouri, and moved to Huntsville, Texas, at the age of 10. After completing her degree in elementary education at LSU in Baton Rouge, Louisiana, she taught elementary school in Arcadia, California, and New York City. After moving to St. Louis, Missouri, in 1966, she devoted her attention to her husband, Garland, and their family of three sons and a daughter.

PHOTO: ANDREA RIEZMAN MARSHALL

Thanks to my family

Chris, Lee, Melissa, Garland, and Keith
for being supportive while I made the quilts.

AQS Books on Quilts

This is only a partial listing of the books on quilts that are available from the American Quilter's Society. AQS books are known the world over for their timely topics, clear writing, beautiful color photographs, and accurate illustrations and patterns. The following books are available from your local bookseller, quilt shop, or public library. If you are unable to locate certain titles in your area, you may order by mail from the AMERICAN QUILTER'S SOCIETY, P.O. Box 3290, Paducah, KY 42002-3290. Add $2.00 for postage for the first book ordered and 40¢ for each additional book. Include item number, title, and price when ordering. Allow 14 to 21 days for delivery. Customers with Visa, MasterCard, or Discover may phone in orders from 7:00–5:00 CST, Monday–Friday, Toll Free 1-800-626-5420.